Business Leadership for IT Projects

For Odette

Business Leadership for IT Projects

GARY LLOYD

Routledge
Taylor & Francis Group

LONDON AND NEW YORK

First published 2013 by Gower Publishing

Published 2016 by Routledge
2 Park Square, Milton Park, Abingdon, Oxfordshire OX14 4RN
711 Third Avenue, New York, NY 10017, USA

First issued in paperback 2016

Routledge is an imprint of the Taylor & Francis Group, an informa business

British Library Cataloguing in Publication Data
A catalogue record for this book is available from the British Library

Library of Congress Cataloging-in-Publication Data
Lloyd, Gary.
 Business leadership for IT projects / by Gary Lloyd.
   pages cm
 Includes bibliographical references and index.
 ISBN 978-1-4094-5690-2 (hbk)
 1. Information technology--Management. 2. Information technology projects--Management. I. Title.
 HD30.2.L66 2014
 004.068′4--dc23

2013006120

ISBN 13: 978-1-138-24640-9 (pbk)
ISBN 13: 978-1-4094-5690-2 (hbk)

Contents

List of Figures

List of Tables

About the Author

Gary Lloyd is a programme and project management specialist who helps organisations and individuals to deliver value from their projects and programmes through: consultancy, mentoring, coaching, training and project assurance. His aim is to work with clients to both lower project risk and to develop organisational and individual delivery capability.

He has been helping businesses to deliver IT enabled change for over 20 years. His roles have ranged from being the business leader who drives the change, through to being a trusted advisor to CEO's and COO's, helping them to get value from their projects, programmes and ventures.

Gary has worked across a variety of countries and cultures that include various European countries, Japan, India, Hong Kong and the USA.

Gary's website can be found at: www.doubleloopconsulting.com and his blog at blog.doubleloopconsulting.com

Acknowledgements

I want to thank four key people for helping to make this book happen.

First, I want to thank my wife Doris. Without her help and encouragement, this book would never have happened. In addition to her unstinting moral support, she was my primary reviewer and acid test for whether my writing made sense and was useful.

Second, I want to thank my friend Stephen Haxby, who read every single word with an eye that combined a critical evaluation of both the big picture and the fine detail. His encouragement gave me the confidence that I could write passably well and had written some useful things. High praise indeed.

Third, I want to thank my friend Mark Alderton, who, through our conversations, provided much of the inspiration for this book. Mark's reviews provided invaluable commentaries on the topics that I wrote about. Many of his ideas found their way into the book.

Finally, I want to thank my commissioning editor, Jonathan Norman, who saw potential in my original proposal and whose enthusiasm lit the touch-paper to complete the project.

Introduction

The track record of IT projects is poor. Less than a third of IT projects deliver what they said they would, on schedule and on budget.[1] The major cause of IT project 'failure' is not, however, poor IT leadership or difficult-to-use technology; it is poor business leadership.[2] Getting value from IT projects is therefore dependent on business managers stepping up to the plate and taking responsibility to lead.

IT people receive substantial amounts of training that is designed to help them to deliver successful projects. That training includes technical, project management and interpersonal skills, and it is usually set within the context of project definition and delivery. Contrast this with the average business manager, who rarely gets any training in how to deliver projects, let alone the special case which is an IT project.

There seems to be an implicit assumption that a business manager who has reached management level should somehow know what do when confronted with an IT project as if it were an innate skill. It's a little like expecting someone to sit behind the wheel of a car for the first time and to be able to drive, just because they happen to be an adult. At least in a car, however, the driver will quickly become aware of his or her lack of competence. But in the complex world of IT projects, the results of bad driving may not manifest themselves for many months or years.

This book sets out to redress this shortfall in business management education. My aim is to help business managers deliver value from their IT projects. You might be a project sponsor, within an organisation, who wants to drive forward a change programme. Or you might be a functional line manager who has been nominated as the 'business representative' on an IT project by your boss. Or you might be a business owner. If you fit any of these descriptions, then this book is for you.

If you are a professional project manager, although the book is not directly addressed to you, it will help you to understand the optimum touchpoints that will maximise the return of investment of a project sponsor or business manager's time. In other words, when and how best to get your project sponsor involved.

I will describe practical tools that you can use at the various stages of a project's life-cycle. If your project is in progress, you can dip into this book and pick out tools that will help to address weaknesses in your project without having to jettison your existing project approach. If, however, you are about to embark on a new project, the tools will provide you with a coherent framework for business involvement in your IT project. Finally, if your organisation or IT supplier already has a well-defined approach to IT projects, you should find that my suggestions complement these approaches by providing a business-centric view.

When I have mentioned the topic of this book to some IT professionals, they have shaken their heads pityingly and said something like 'of course you realise that there is no such thing as an IT project?'. They are anxious to show that they understand that the delivery of an IT system achieves nothing, unless it is coupled with the achievement of a business outcome. And of course they are right. However, I never hear the same semantic point from business managers. They well understand the challenge of getting value from an 'IT project'. But to avoid doubt about what makes IT projects distinctive, let me offer my definition. You will also find it, and other terms, in the glossary at the back of this book.

WHAT IS AN IT PROJECT?

An IT project is a project that delivers a new or changed capability, based on IT, that delivers business value. The project is not complete until the value is realised or demonstrably on the way to being realised.

Research shows that most IT projects succeed or fail because of people rather than because of technology issues. The vast majority of projects are simply not at the cutting edge of technology. I have therefore described a framework that combines a strong sense of process with a strong sense of 'people factors'. The aim has been to integrate what we know from the study of psychology into the overall approach and tools described, such that the tools address process and people needs simultaneously.

The psychological aspects have been greatly informed by the work of the Nobel Prize winner Daniel Kahneman and the cognitive neuroscientist Tali Sharot. Kahneman's book, *Thinking Fast and Slow*,[3] explores how we really make judgements and decisions. It pulls together most of the key research from the last 30 years, including his own. The mind, says Kahneman, is 'a machine for jumping to conclusions'. We fix on a plausible story as soon as we can, then set about collecting facts to support that story and rejecting those that do not. This will sound familiar to anyone who has seen an IT project go off in the wrong direction or entirely off the rails.

Tali Sharot's book, *The Optimism Bias*,[4] is based on her research into how people deal with traumatic events. She concludes that human beings are innately optimistic for good evolutionary reasons. We are wired to believe that the future will be better than the past, even when this is contradicted by the evidence. In particular, we are likely to believe that our own personal outcomes will be better than those of individuals faced with the same situations and resources. The resulting overconfidence pervades IT projects.

IT projects have a particular characteristic that exacerbates the problems described by Kahneman and Sharot. That characteristic is the difficulty of unambiguously defining the final product. One, increasingly predominant, school of thought argues that an exact definition of the final product just isn't possible for something as intangible as a software system. Rather, it is argued that IT projects should be journeys of discovery that take advantage of the 'softness' characteristic that accommodates change more readily than a project whose product is made from of steel, concrete and glass. But whether you subscribe to this school of thought or not, most IT practitioners will agree that the process from gathering requirements through to realisation is a major challenge for many IT projects.

The tools in this book aim to address the psychological bear-traps described by Kahneman and Sharot in two ways: first, by finding ways to slow down our thinking, in order to give the more evolved aspects of our brains an opportunity to join the conversation; and, second, by soliciting outside views that offer different perspectives and less emotional involvement in the process or outcome.

So let me start by slowing down your thinking straight away. If you have an existing project, take my one-minute health-check on the next page. If your project hasn't yet started, use the health-check to think about how you might answer in three months' time … and beware your optimism bias. If the questions, or indeed your answers, make you feel a little queasy, then you will find the rest of this book to be very useful.

THE ONE-MINUTE HEALTH-CHECK

1. How much customer or stakeholder value has been delivered so far?
2. How many of the critical business case assumptions have been validated?
3. What proportion of the budget has been used to achieve this?

What about over the coming month or three months?

1

Don't Do IT

IT projects are usually expensive and slow to deliver relative to other business changes and operational costs (see below). More often than not, they fail to deliver their expected value at close to anything like the estimated budget and schedule. This chapter aims to make you aware of how frequently IT projects go wrong and, before you commit to an IT project, gives you some common scenarios where the risk and cost of an IT project is not the only option.

If you are already committed to an IT project, you might think that it is too late to reconsider. But once you have read this chapter, think about how much is yet to be spent on your project. Use the one minute-health-check given in the Introduction and evaluate whether the money yet to be spent is likely to get you the value you want.

IT Projects Usually Exceed their Cost and Time Estimates

THE STANDISH GROUP SURVEY OF 70,000 PROJECTS

The most often quoted studies into overruns and their causes come from the Standish Group, whose first report was published in 1995.[1] It was based on replies from 365 respondents, covering 8,380 projects, mainly in the USA, and it reported that:

- 31 per cent of projects were cancelled before they were completed (classified as 'impaired');

- 53 per cent cost 189 per cent of their estimates (classified as 'challenged');

- just 16 per cent were delivered on time and on budget (classified as 'successful').

The report also stated that in large companies, completed projects contained only 42 per cent of their originally proposed features. The figures were better in small companies, with 78 per cent of projects delivering 74 per cent of their originally proposed features. The report concluded that: 'Software development projects are in chaos'. The report was named 'the CHAOS Report' (no-one seems to remember why the word 'chaos' was in upper case, but it has been retained ever since).

Since 1995, the Standish Group has run its survey annually and has developed a subscription service for its data and its advice on best practices, which are derived from that data. By 2010, the CHAOS Report had become the *CHAOS Manifesto*,[2] with '15 years of data on why projects succeed and fail, representing 70,000 completed IT projects' originating from respondents worldwide. At the time of writing, the latest available figures on 'success and failure' come from projects surveyed in 2008 and reported in 2010. These show that:

- 24 per cent of projects were cancelled (either prior to completion or were never used);

- 44 per cent were late, overbudget and/or with less than the required number of features and functions;

- 32 per cent delivered required features and functions on time and on budget.

As the figures are better than 1996, you might be tempted to conclude that things are slowly improving. Unfortunately, the improvement in performance from 1995 to 2008 masks the fact that 2008's figures represent what the Standish Group calls 'the highest failure rate in over a decade'.

The Standish Group's interpretation of its data is not without its critics. The January/February 2010 issue of *IEEE Software* magazine carried an article entitled 'The Rise and Fall of the Chaos Report Figures'.[3] It was written by Professor Chris Verhoef and PhD student J. Laurenz Eveleens, at the time in Vrije Universitiet Amsterdam's Department of Computer Science. Their main criticism seems to relate to the way in which the Standish Group classifies projects as failures or successes. They argue that classifying a project as a failure because it exceeds its budget or schedule is meaningless if the original estimates of cost, schedule and functionality were poor in the first place. They go on to say that:

> *The part of a project's success that's related to estimation deviation is highly context dependent. In some contexts 25% estimation error*

does no harm and doesn't impact what would normally impact project
success. In other contexts, only 5% overrun would cause much harm.

This is all well and good, but it is scant consolation for business managers who have to use estimates of cost, schedule and functionality to justify projects in their business cases.

But in any event, the 2010 *CHAOS Manifesto* only uses the term 'failure' for projects that were cancelled or delivered something that was never used. Other projects are classified as either 'challenged' or 'successful'. Their classification criteria might have been looser in previous years, but whether a project that exceeds its budget by 25 per cent is a failure or not seems a little academic. The data still says that only a third of projects deliver what was expected on time and on budget.

The other (private) criticism I have heard is that because the Standish Group is selling a service based on its data that advises clients how to achieve better project outcomes, it has a vested interest in painting a dire picture. This begs the question as to whether independent research supports the Standish Group's conclusions. The answer is yes it does, and it comes from the British Computer Society and the Saïd Business School at the University of Oxford.

THE BRITISH COMPUTER SOCIETY

The British Computer Society (BCS) is the UK's professional body for IT. In 2008, it published the results of research that looked a 214 projects, covering the period 1998–2005, across a range of sectors within the European Union.[4] The findings are summarised in Figure 1.1 on the following page. An overrun represents a schedule or cost overrun or both.

The figures show that 24 per cent of projects were cancelled after significant expenditure. This is exactly the same figure reported by the Standish Group. It also shows that 44 per cent of projects were delivered on time and to budget, a better performance than the 32 per cent reported by the Standish Group, though not a million miles away and hardly a cause for celebration.

What really jumped out at me, however, was that 23 per cent of projects overran their budget by 70 per cent or more. Add in the 24 per cent of projects that were cancelled after significant money was spent and pretty close to half of the projects went very badly wrong.

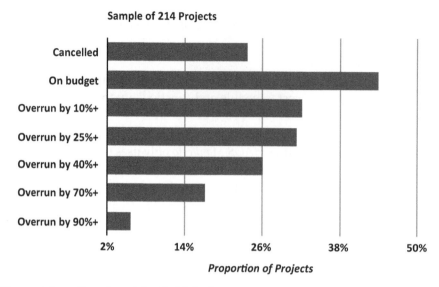

Figure 1.1   Results of the British Computer Society survey of project failure

Note: The overrun bars are cumulative, such that 'overrun by 10%+' includes all of those projects that have overrun by 10 per cent or more, so it includes those projects that have overrun by 25 per cent, 40 per cent, 70 per cent and 90 per cent. Similarly, 'overrun by 25%+' includes projects that overrun by 40 per cent, 70 per cent, 90 per cent and so on for the other bars.

This bleak assessment is further supported by the most recent research from the Saïd Business School.

THE SAÏD BUSINESS SCHOOL

The September 2011 issue of *Harvard Business Review* published an article entitled 'Why Your IT Project May Be Riskier Than You Think'.[5] It was co-authored by Bent Flyvbjerg, the Professor and Chair of Major Programme Management at the Saïd Business School.

The article reported the initial findings of a study of 1,471 projects worldwide. It found that the average project budget overrun was only 27 per cent, but that:

> *Fully one in six of the projects we studied was a black swan, with a cost overrun of 200 per cent, on average, and a schedule overrun of almost 70 per cent.*

This tells us that we should expect most of our IT projects to overrun. Sometimes, however, they will overrun massively. Note that the 200 per cent figure is the magnitude of the overrun, such that a £5 million budget turns into a £15 million cost. You might wonder how a project can become 200 per cent overbudget without someone pulling the plug. Unfortunately, the article doesn't address this question, but in my experience it is a combination of reasons. Foremost is the belief that so much money has been spent so far that it would be a waste to 'give up now, with the end in sight'. Unfortunately, the end often remains in sight for a considerable amount of time but never arrives.

Incidentally, the term 'black swan' comes from Nassim Nicholas Taleb's book *The Black Swan: The Impact of the Highly Improbable.*[6] Taleb describes a black swan as an event that is 'outside the realm of regular expectations … carries an extreme impact … [and is] after the fact explainable and predictable'. This definition will sound very familiar to anyone who has been close to a significant IT project disaster.

Here are three (of many) examples:

- British retailer Sainsbury's 'Warehouse Automation' project made it into production in 2003, but was later scrapped in 2005, with a reported write-off of £260 million.[7]

- The Federal Bureau of Investigation's 'Virtual Case File' Project was written off after an expenditure of $170 million in 2005.[8]

- In July 2006, the CEO of Anglo-French Clearing House LCH. Clearnet departed when his company wrote off €47.8m after scrapping a failed three-year project to build an integrated clearing platform.[9]

Can You Defy the Statistics?

Taken together, the studies summarised above tell us that a majority of IT projects overrun, usually by 25 per cent or more, and sometimes when they go wrong, they go very badly wrong. Some people argue that this is simply a question of estimating error. But if your business case depends on the estimate and the project turns out to cost twice as much as you thought it would, then that's pretty serious.

So, do you believe the statistics? If you are like most people, you will fall into one of two camps, depending on whether you are observing someone else's project or whether it is your own project, setting out to achieve an important business outcome. The first time I pulled together this data was for a talk to a class of MBA undergraduates. I had a slide prepared that said something like: 'Only 32 per cent of IT projects deliver what was wanted, on time and budget – one in six overrun by 200 per cent or more'. I was ready to shock them.

'So', I asked them, 'what proportion of IT projects do you think deliver what was expected on time and budget?' I moved to the flip-chart to plot the distribution of their answers. 'Zero', someone shouted. I laughed. 'Five per cent', shouted another person. My laugh got a bit more nervous, as my presentation storyline evaporated. The final consensus of the 80 or so business students was that no more than 10 per cent of projects deliver what is needed to schedule and budget. When it's not our project, we are very pessimistic about IT projects.

We seem transformed when it is our own project; that innate optimism bias described by Tali Sharot[10] kicks in. Like most car drivers, we believe that accidents will not happen to us because we are better than average drivers. Accidents happen to other people because they are careless and, let's be honest, not as smart as we are. Studies show that people have a problem applying statistical generalisations to themselves. Perversely, however, we tend to generalise from very few personal experiences, be they good or bad.[11]

So, do you believe you can defy the statistics? Is there really no alternative to an IT project? Let me throw in one last statistic about project size from the Standish Group before considering some common scenarios that beg for an alternative. In its database of 70,000 projects, the Group found that projects with a staff cost of:

- less than $750,000 have a 71 per cent chance of coming in on time and on budget;

- between $750,000 and $3 million have a 38 per cent of coming in on time and on budget;

- over $10 million have a two per cent chance of coming in on time and on budget.

This chimes with research that I carried out earlier in my career. I found that the productivity of IT project teams declined exponentially as project size increases.

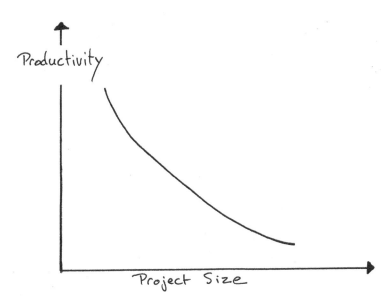

Figure 1.2   Productivity versus project size

Small is definitely beautiful when it comes to IT projects. In Chapter 4 I will be recommending that you break your projects down into chunks, each of which delivers usable value.

Seriously Considering Alternatives

The sections that follow illustrate some common scenarios where an IT project could have been avoided, or at least minimised, to a great extent.

AVOIDING THE COST OF BUYING A SERVICE

I was once asked to rescue a project in trouble. It had a 'fixed deadline' and the project manager gave it a 70 per cent chance of being delivered on time. This was actually his way of saying that it would not deliver on time. I was asked by the business executive responsible to 'take over the project and drive it to a successful conclusion'. I asked the executive about the project drivers and he was a bit sketchy, which made me somewhat suspicious. I agreed to undertake an assessment of the project before deciding whether to take on the role.

I discovered that the project came about because a supplier of essential business data had proposed a 50 per cent price increase for the service.

Needless to say, everyone in the client company was mightily irritated. At a brainstorming session a couple of days after the increase was proposed, one of the IT team suggested that the company could develop its own solution to replace the vendor service. After a short discussion, the meeting concluded that a home-grown service could be up and running before the supplier contract expired in five months' time.

The replacement project missed this deadline, necessitating an expensive six-month contract extension with the supplier. And now, at the time that I became involved, there was a danger that it would not be ready before the extension expired.

There were a multitude of reasons why the project was not going to be ready and many could be addressed. But these problems were all par for the course. The hard truth was that although the price increase was a bitter pill to swallow, it was always going to be cheaper than building (and, don't forget, maintaining) a home-grown solution.

A lot of projects are created to avoid the costs of buying a service because the service seems expensive. If, however, you take into account the project cost, the risk of overrun and the operational costs of building and running your own solution, you will often find that buying is cheaper. In this example, the decision by the company to build its own solution was an emotional rather than a logical one; something which is not uncommon.

Something else that is a common justification for an IT project is the belief that 'our business is a bit different from other people's, so we need our own solution'. This is rarely the case, as most shrink-wrapped services represent best practice processes. It's usually cheaper to bend your own business processes to a packaged solution than to build your own. The common retort to this assertion is that home-grown software gives the company a competitive advantage. But that is just for the vast majority of business processes.[12]

THE LURE OF SEAMLESS INTEGRATION AND SYNCHRONISED DATA

It's clearly a good thing for data to move seamlessly from one system to another, without human intervention. It is less error-prone and faster than doing it manually. In addition, many organisations have islands of similar, often customer-related, data. Synchronising these data is self-evidently a good thing. But what if the cost of automation is high or uncertain and the cost of errors is relatively low?

In 1999, a friend of mine got the job as Operations Director at a large US-based investment bank. Her key goal was to reduce annual costs by 15 per cent. She knew that projects were a big expense but that they are also the way through which one reduces cost. Her first act, therefore, was to commission a review of all the projects that were under way.

One of the projects had an estimated cost close to $3 million and a duration of 11 months. It was already running overbudget and looked likely to come in late. The goal of the project was to ensure that four separate back-office systems stored consistent data. The project aimed to fulfil this goal by linking together the four different systems. It was an elegant IT solution, using the latest communications technology and protocols.

During a brainstorming session designed to try to get the project back on track, a junior operations manager suggested that the project be replaced with three junior staff. They could, he argued, check and correct the data manually. Errors would be minimised by cross-checking each other's work. Only two people would really be needed but a third was sensible to act as cover for holidays and sickness. But people were in love with the elegance of the IT based solution and believed that the goal of 'straight through processing' was reason enough in itself to justify the project. The suggestion was dismissed as 'silly'.

But the manager was a graduate trainee, unfamiliar with corporate ways, so he buttonholed my friend at a staff meeting. He pointed out that the cost of the three staff, to achieve the same outcome as the project, would be around $100,000 year. Even without sophisticated accounting, it was clear that it would take about 10 years before the IT project showed a saving over the manual option – assuming the IT project didn't overrun! The mental arithmetic caused her to pause just long enough for him produce a sheet of paper on which he had also calculated the cost of errors. Some errors would still get through, he argued, but the ability to eliminate them completely wasn't worth the cost of the IT project.

Despite this unusual approach, the next week, the bank hired three high-school graduates who were keen to get into investment banking. They all turned up for their first day in jeans and trainers. Thereafter, my friend always insisted that every project proposal had to include a 'Sneakerware' option.

AUTOMATING LOW-FREQUENCY TRANSACTIONS

I have seen a lot of examples of IT projects that have automated low-frequency transactions at a cost that far outweighs a less sophisticated or manual solution. Sometimes, as in the previous example, the project is created simply because there is a belief that everything should, as far as possible, be integrated, or sometimes it is in anticipation of transaction volumes whose probability is very low.

I recall a project in a major UK financial institution that planned to spend around £3 million on a risk management system. The volume of transactions for existing customers was such that the required solution could have been constructed, and easily maintained, on a small spreadsheet. The rationale was that a purpose-built, automated solution was better per se than an error-prone spreadsheet (which is true) and that a new system could be scaled, almost infinitely, to take on new customers.

The problem with this justification was that there were no plans to recruit more than a few new customers for whom the risk management system would be needed. The customers in this instance were institutional investors who were expensive to recruit and expensive to service. The organisation didn't want to dump its existing customers, for relationship reasons, but this wasn't a business it was looking to develop, aside from a few key relationships.

However, the project was, frankly, more exciting than the day job and afforded the opportunity to play around with some new technology. The head of the risk department embraced the project as a symbol of his department's willingness to embrace change. And when the project started to run into trouble, he seemed to see it as a test of his virility to get it delivered. The project eventually cost over £4 million and was nearly six months late. A spreadsheet functioned without problem, in the interim, and the new system is, apparently, a bit slow and difficult to use.

BUSINESS PROCESS REDESIGN DOESN'T NEED IT

Something else that happens quite frequently is that businesses don't review and redesign their business processes until they have decided to implement a new IT system. It can often turn out that the business process changes that deliver the project's value could have been ushered in by relatively minor changes to existing systems. You can therefore often minimise the degree of

IT change, and hence the risk, if you ask the team to generate zero or low-cost options, focusing on process redesign. I will return to this theme in Chapter 5.

NEW BUSINESS PROCESSES AUTOMATED TOO SOON

Another common scenario is seeking to fully automate a new business process before that process is mature and well understood. This typically happens when a business introduces a new product or service. It also sometimes occurs with start-ups. There is an understandable desire to want the new process to be properly supported by technology in order to provide the best product or service possible.

But choosing to fully automate too early can have a couple of unwanted consequences. First, the business can get locked into a process embodied in the software that is difficult to adapt as the business' understanding of customers' needs evolve. Second, the business tries to anticipate future needs and ends up paying for lots of features that will never be used. The alternative is to automate lightly and use sneakerware until the need is really well understood, unless you are really confident that volumes are going to accelerate very quickly.

Do You Really Need to Do IT?

Ask yourself these questions:

- Can you change the business process in some way without the change involving IT?

- Can you employ agency staff who will cost less than an IT project?

- Is there a supplier who will provide a turnkey service at a predictable cost?

- Can you combine small IT changes with one or more of the above?

The record of IT projects is so patchy that you should seriously consider these questions before deciding to embark on a significant IT project. Revisit the drivers of the project. Revisit the assumptions that underpin both the problem and the solution. Do so with the perspective of a business owner whose own money is at stake rather than that of an employee.

If you have done all this and have still concluded that you need an IT project to achieve your goals, then welcome to the rest of the book. I hope it will make your journey easier.

Key Points from this Chapter

- IT projects usually exceed their forecast and schedule, and deliver less than expected.

- Some projects will overrun by more than 100 per cent.

- You are probably being over-optimistic about your own projects and need to factor this into your thinking.

- Seriously consider non-IT solutions, particularly business process changes, as an alternative.

2

Stepping Up to the Plate

In the previous chapter, we looked at the frequency with which IT projects go wrong. In this chapter, we will examine the reasons why IT projects go wrong and what you can do about it.

From collating the available research and using my own experience, my conclusion is that poor business leadership is the primary reason that IT projects don't deliver value. That's good news for you because your ability to influence your project outcome, through your actions, is disproportionate when compared to any other possible success factors such as technology platform choices. But it's also bad news because the onus is on you to take responsibility and to take action.

We'll start by looking at the common frustrations felt by business managers. We will then look at the underlying causes of these frustrations before defining what I mean by taking leadership. If you only read one chapter of this book, make it this one. Everything else in the book is designed to support the goal of taking leadership.

Common Frustrations with IT Projects

This book was prompted by hearing business managers complain, often emotionally, about their frustrations with IT projects. So, when I came to write this book, I decided to talk to as many business managers as I could in order to get their views on why IT projects fail to deliver value. During 2012, I surveyed 57 people, talked to another 26 face to face and ran three focus groups.

It seemed natural to start the face-to-face conversations and focus groups with what, in their direct experience, commonly went wrong and then try to drill down into why. But the topic of what went wrong proved to be like a conversational magnet. Every time I moved the discussion on to why things went wrong, they indulged me briefly before returning to a long list of frustrations.

An online survey, as part of this exercise, elicited a similar reaction. The free-form text responses about what went wrong were overflowing with frustrations. In contrast, most of the responses to the questions about why things went wrong would only have one or two responses, often accompanied by a list of additional frustrations or a reiteration of those already described using a different form of words.

Below are the most commonly articulated frustrations:

1.   Benefits not realised.

2.   Cost and time overruns.

3.   Lack of can-do attitude from the IT supplier.

4.   Mismatch between business requirements and solution provided.

5.   Inflexibility of the IT supplier in terms of:

    a)   process – 'this is how we will do it';
    b)   technology – a desire to use what's new and fashionable;
    c)   solution – an inability to think outside the box;
    d)   terminology – hiding behind jargon rather than using plain English.

From the tone of the comments, it was clear that the majority of people blamed their IT supplier for their frustrations. This wasn't a surprising result. It was consistent with the views that I had heard throughout my career. (This is probably an appropriate time to mention that when I use the term 'IT supplier' in this book, it could be an internal IT department, an external services supplier or a combination of both.)

In parallel to this informal research into causes, I pulled together what research I could find into the underlying causes of IT project problems, and these are summarised in the next section.

The Top Five Causes of IT Project Malfunction

If you search the Web, you will find a lot of information written about the causes of IT project malfunction. It is, however, rarely possible to perform a definitive autopsy on an IT project. Much of what is written is subjective opinion, particularly when it comes from management consultancies. They have a tendency to publish seemingly definitive lists of causes based on what their clients tell them in general conversations about work.

I have therefore excluded these lists from my consolidation of causes and stuck to research where there has been a specific effort to determine the reasons why IT projects go wrong. Here are the sources that I used to come up with the most common causes of problems:

1. The *CHAOS Manifesto* produced by the Standish Group (2010):[1] a survey of 70,000 specifically focused on why IT projects go wrong and the most comprehensive source of data.

2. The British Computer Society findings (reported in Chapter 1) for 214 projects, covering the period 1998–2005, across a range of sectors within the European Union (2008).[2]

3. The findings of the Organisational Aspects Special Interest Group (OASIG), which is supported by the UK government and interviewed 45 experts from consultancies and universities about 'project failure' (1995).[3]

4. A list of 'Common Causes of Failure' for government projects jointly published by two UK government agencies: the Office of Government Commerce (OGC) and the National Audit Office (NAO) (1995).[4] These causes were reiterated in 2003 in a report to Parliament, entitled *Government IT Projects*, produced by the Parliamentary Office of Science and Technology.[5]

5. Schmidt, Lyytinen, Keil and Cule asked three panels of experienced project managers in Hong Kong, Finland and the USA to rank the most significant project risk factors (2001).[6]

6. The findings published by KPMG Canada based on a survey of 176 projects (1997).[7]

7. The findings of a survey of executives' views on 'business transformation' conducted by Cap Gemini, including a section entitled 'Reasons for transformation success and failure' (2007).[8] The survery was not strictly about IT failure but had a strong IT theme, as you would expect from Cap Gemini.

The following is my synthesis of the main reasons why projects go wrong.

THE TOP FIVE CAUSES OF PROJECT MALFUNCTION

1. Unclear business objectives and links to strategic priorities.
2. Lack of executive and senior management support.
3. Poor quality and changing requirements.
4. Lack of user involvement.
5. Poor planning and risk management.

With the possible exception of the last item, these causes point to one thing: poor business leadership. It is the business that has the capability to address all of these points, including the last one.

Interestingly, IT professionals go in for an enormous amount of breast beating, challenging themselves to do a better job at engaging with 'the business' and getting good-quality requirements. They believe that the onus is on them to drag what they need out of business managers in order to get the job done. But why should it be that way? Shouldn't business managers be agonising about how they can ensure that they get what they want?

Examples of Poor Business Leadership

Only the most spectacular of 'failures' of private companies make their way into the public domain. Most like to forget about projects that have failed to deliver against their business cases and move on. Failures only become visible when the magnitude of a failure is so large that it has to be acknowledged in the company's annual report with a project write-off that hits the bottom line. Even then, we rarely find out the real reasons for these failures because there is no incentive to make them public.

This is not surprising, given the first two causes in the list above. Together they can be summarised in one word: leadership. It is bad enough that shareholders find out about failures. Admitting that the failure occurred because of a lack of leadership at the most senior levels would require a resignation letter alongside such an admission; it is easier to blame the technology or the supplier.

Large public sector projects are different. Their failures attract attention when the estimated expenditure starts to go through the roof, making them visible to public accounts committees. And when this happens, there is, in many countries, a public examination of the causes by a government agency or committee of elected representatives.

These spectacular failures may seem to be a world away from more modestly sized IT projects but, size apart, the pitfalls are the same. IT projects run late and overspend one day at a time. They share the same susceptibility to the thinking that 'it would be a waste to give up now with the end in sight'. They spend yet more money trying to salvage the project, often throwing good money after bad.

Recall Nassim Nicholas Taleb's definition of a black swan as an event that is 'outside the realm of regular expectations ... carries an extreme impact ... [and is] after the fact explainable and predictable'. An IT project doesn't have to overspend by tens of millions to qualify; it depends on the wealth of your organisation. A £10 million project that ends up costing between £20 million and $30 million is a black swan. But a £1 million project that ends up £2 million or £3 million is also a black swan. And a £100,000 project that ends up costing between £200,000 and £300,000 may well be regarded as a black swan in your organisation. Keep this in mind when you read the three examples that follow. The causes are common to all IT projects, regardless of the magnitude of the numbers.

THE FBI VIRTUAL CASE FILE PROJECT

In 2005, the FBI scrapped its project to automate the management of investigation information, writing off $170 million. Glenn A. Fine, the US Department of Justice's Inspector General, told the Senate Committee on Appropriations that the originally estimated cost of $380 million had ballooned to $581 million.[9] He concluded that, given that the project had already cost $170 million, he was 'not confident that the FBI has a firm sense of how much longer and how much more it will cost to develop and deploy a usable system'.

In his report, Fine made the following conclusions:

- 'The main responsibility for the failure rests with the FBI', not the IT supplier.

- The FBI engaged its supplier:

  - 'without providing or insisting upon defined requirements;
  - specific milestones;
  - critical decision review points; and
  - penalties for poor contractor performance'.

- 'Requirements kept changing'.[10]

That this was a failure of business leadership is without doubt and not without parallel in many smaller projects.

THE NHS DETAILED CARE RECORDS PROJECT

The goal of this project was to create a central database of clinical records for National Health Service (NHS) patients. The aim was to replace the existing system of locally held, often paper-based records. For example, when my mother was undergoing treatment for lung cancer, she visited five different London hospitals because each had different expertise or equipment. At each hospital she was asked for the same basic information, usually by a nurse, including her name and address and the medication she was taking. Each hospital also took the same x-rays and blood tests because, they said, these were likely to get lost being physically transferred between hospitals. So the potential benefits of the project are clear. It was actually very similar to the FBI project – maybe they should have talked?

In the UK, ultimate public scrutiny is conducted by the Public Accounts Committee, a committee of elected Members of Parliament. In 2011, the Committee published its conclusions and recommendations regarding the Detailed Care Records Project as part of 'The National Programme for IT in the National Health Service (NHS)'.[11] Its conclusions were that:

- 'weak management and oversight of the Programme have resulted in poor accountability for project performance';

- the project 'has been unable to deliver its original aim'; and

- the project 'was unable to show what had been achieved for the £2.7 billion spent to date'.

Now, actually, this doesn't say too much about causes, but can 'weak management and oversight' mean anything other than 'business' management when the price tag is in billions of pounds?

THE SAINSBURY'S WAREHOUSE AUTOMATION PROJECT

To complete this excursion into schadenfreude, I thought I should include a private sector black swan. Because it is a private sector disaster, the reasons for failure were not made public, but I think that we can infer some key problems which have important lessons for any IT project.

In 2004, UK food retailing giant Sainsbury's reported its first ever half-year loss of £39 million when it wrote off £260 million of IT expenditure. The new system had made it into production but proved to be unworkable. Four newly automated warehouses were closed and Sainsbury had to take on 3,000 staff to stock shelves.[12]

The project began in 2000 when the new CEO, Sir Peter Davis, arrived and launched 'The Business Transformation Programme'. The key planks of the four-year programme were supply chain management, Electronic Point of Sale (EPOS) and the outsourcing of IT to Accenture.[13] The warehouse automation project was at the heart of the supply chain management overhaul. Three years later, Davis reported that the Business Transformation Programme was on track and had delivered cumulative savings of around £700 million. The Accenture contract was to be extended for an additional three years.[14]

In March 2004, Davis moved up to the role of Chairman and Justin King was appointed as the new CEO. Davis was due to serve as Chairman until July 2005, but left in June 2004. In October 2004, it was Justin King who broke the bad news about the loss.[15] The announcement resulted in an unseemly row between Sainsbury and Accenture. Accenture released a statement saying that 'IT automation systems within Sainsbury's four new automated depots are not, and never have been under the scope of the existing contract'.[16] The £2.16 billion, 10-year outsourcing contract with Accenture was terminated a year later.[17]

The key questions that this raises in my mind are, first, how does one get three years into a programme before finding out that an essential part of the solution is not fit for purpose? Second, how does the CEO find himself giving a rosy presentation of progress when things are going pear-shaped in the background? We don't have the answers to this, but there are some lessons that can be learned. Business managers need to:

- establish a culture that accepts bad news about project progress;

- engage with IT suppliers to understand the key business and IT risks and design a delivery strategy to tackle them as early as possible;

- keep close to the project throughout, ensuring that assumptions are validated, risks are managed and progress is properly monitored;

- remember that value is a combination of benefit and cost.

Stepping Up to the Plate

Business managers get involved in IT projects in a variety of ways. Sometimes it is because you, as a business manager, want to get something done. Sometimes it is because someone else wants to get something done, but doesn't have the time to get personally involved and has nominated you to represent them. Or it may be that you are going to be affected by the change, as a victim or beneficiary of the project, and you want to keep a watchful eye on it.

If your organisation or IT supplier has a development or project management methodology, you might be asked to slot into the project with the title of something like:

- Business Owner.

- Project Sponsor.

- Executive.

- Senior User.

- Business Change Manager.

- Steering Committee Member.

- Programme or Project Board Member.

There is nothing wrong with taking on one of these roles for the sake of good project governance. However, what I have often seen is that when business managers assume one of these titles, they lose sight of their broader role: that of customer. Busy with their day jobs, they fall into a thinking trap that says:

> *These guys seem to know what they are doing, they have a process and I have a role within it which has a description. I'll climb into that comfy seat, do what is asked of me and attend these regular meetings they have set up that let me know how it's going. If they need me, I'm sure they'll let me know.*

With the assignment of a project role title, Business managers transform from demanding drivers into passive passengers. Whatever formal role you take in the project's governance structure, always think of yourself as the customer. It doesn't matter whether you are a junior or senior member of the business team; you are a customer of the IT supplier. When you attend a meeting or read some documentation, try to remind yourself that you are a customer.

THINK OF YOURSELF AS THE CUSTOMER OF YOUR IT SUPPLIER

Whatever formal role you take in the project's governance structure, always think of yourself a customer. How would you behave if you were spending your own money having your dream home built, rather than an IT system? How demanding and involved would you be to ensure you get what you want?

The language that we use to describe things has an impact on how we think and act. This is because when we use a particular term, it instantly fires up a network of subconscious associations.[18] So, if you say to yourself 'I am the customer' and *believe it*, your will subconsciously take on the behaviours that you exhibit when you buy more mundane products. Think about buying a computer or a car:

- The supplier is providing you with a product.

- You want to ensure you get what you want.

- You want get value for money.

- You want to ask questions about what you are getting.

- You don't want to go away with the wrong thing.

- You consider some different options before choosing.

- You try out options whenever possible.

- You are responsible for the choice, not the supplier.

These are the sorts of things that customers do. Of course, buying a car is not the same as initiating an IT project, but the customer mindset should be the same. Be a demanding customer. Don't be like the diner who doesn't want to send back their over-salted soup because they 'don't want to make a fuss'. Being a demanding customer for an IT project means taking the lead and asking questions about what you are going to get. Ask your supplier the following questions:

- How can I help you and your team understand the problem we are trying to solve?

- How can I help you and your team understand the way in which the project creates value?

- How can I be sure that I am going to get what we agreed?

- How are you going to ensure that it works the way I want it to?

- How can I avoid leaving it to the last minute to find out whether it meets my expectations?

- How can I help reduce the risk of cost and schedule overruns?

- How can I understand progress in order to know whether we are on target?

In the chapters that follow, I will advise you how to best get these answers and more. But what is more important than specific questions is taking on the mindset, internalising it and behaving that way *throughout* the project. Stepping up to the plate and taking responsibility for the project outcome is the single most important piece of advice in this book.

> **STEPPING UP TO THE PLATE**
>
> If you want to get value from your IT project, you have to take responsibility for its outcome. Hoping that it will turn out OK is not enough. You need to take action.

The Role of the Project Sponsor

Before discussing the different ways that business managers get involved in IT projects, I want to set the context by talking about the role of the project sponsor. Most people understand what is meant by the project sponsor. This is the person who wants the project done and who usually holds the purse-strings. Some project management methodologies use the term 'project executive', but it is essentially the same thing.

Although I think the role is well understood, I have seen some debate recently about the role and responsibilities of the project sponsor, so to avoid misunderstandings, here is the definition of project sponsor that I intend to use in this book.

> **THE PROJECT SPONSOR IS THE PERSON WHO:**
> - Wants the value delivered by the project.
> - Has agreed to spend the money to get that value.
> - Will champion the project throughout its life.
> - Will help the project team address obstacles outside their control.
> - Will engage fully at the key touchpoints (see the next section and Chapter 7).
> - Has the power to stop the project if it is not going to deliver the expected value.

The last of these points will not be in everyone's definition, but I think it is a good test of whether the sponsor has sufficient decision-making authority, with respect to the project, to be an effective sponsor. Ideally, the sponsor will be someone senior who has the time to take an active leadership role, including the ability to influence stakeholders, some of whom are likely to be peers.

However, he or she also needs to have the time to take an active leadership role, as described in the following chapters. I once worked in an organisation where the Chief Operating Officer (COO) was designated as the sponsor for almost all IT projects. However, the COO was way too senior to get actively involved in most of the projects and this left a vacuum in terms of business leadership, leaving many projects effectively rudderless.

If a senior person is not going to have time to fulfil his or her role in the project properly, it is better to appoint someone more junior who will be fully engaged. This will only work if the person appointed as sponsor is genuinely enthusiastic about and supportive of the project. And, critically, it is essential that he or she is empowered to make decisions that are not second-guessed later. If the person nominated as sponsor has to continually check with someone 'upstairs', he or she will not be effective in the role or taken seriously by the project team.

Appointing someone more junior does bring with it the disadvantage of that person not having sufficient authority in the eyes of senior stakeholders. On balance, however, it is better than having a sponsor who drifts in and out. An approach that I have seen work is to have a junior-ranking sponsor who is supported by a more senior 'project owner' who can help with stakeholder management. The 'project owner' is analogous to the company chairman and the 'sponsor' to the CEO. At the risk of repeating myself, there is no point in adopting this approach if the 'owner' is seen as the 'the real project sponsor'. The test of this is whether the sponsor is empowered to make decisions that stick. But like a good CEO, he or she is likely to consult with the chairman when there are particularly big decisions to make.

Getting sponsorship right is crucial. A while ago, I ran a poll on the LinkedIn group for programme managers/directors. I asked:

> To what extent does the project-based experience and capability of a project sponsor have an impact on the overall outcome of a project?

The results were as follows:

- Not at all: 0 per cent.

- Hardly at all: 4 per cent.

- To some extent: 24 per cent.

- To a great extent: 32 per cent.

- Absolutely critical: 38 per cent.[19]

This is not a huge sample, but these are senior people who run programmes and projects, so they should have a good perspective on the situation. This view about the importance of sponsorship is supported by our old friends the Standish Group and its 70,000 project database. In a blog post, Jennifer Lynch, the group's Communications Director, wrote:

> *We believe improvement in the skills of the executive sponsor is the single most important factor that will increase project success.*[20]

Your Role in the Project

There are three main ways in which business managers usually become involved in IT projects:

1.   You want to get something done.

2.   Someone else wants to get something done, but doesn't have the time to get personally involved and has nominated you to represent them.

3.   You are going to be affected by the change, as a victim or beneficiary of the project, and you want to keep a watchful eye on it.

If you fall into the first category, you are either the project sponsor or you have lobbied effectively to convince someone more senior to sponsor the project. If you are the project sponsor, then, as I said in the previous section, you will need to ensure that you have the time to provide leadership. Others are unlikely to share your enthusiasm for the project, so you need to be personally involved. There are a number of touchpoints that require your leadership and therefore your time. These are set out below and provide the structure for this book.

If the project is important but you do not think that you will have the time to lead it, appoint someone you trust as the sponsor and delegate decision-making authority to them. Rebrand yourself as the project 'owner', but take great care not to undermine your sponsor. Similarly, if you are in the first category but are not the sponsor, you either need to convince the sponsor to get involved personally or to delegate decision-making authority to you as the person who understands and is committed to the project.

BUSINESS LEADERSHIP TOUCHPOINTS
- Defining a problem, need or mission.
- Defining a shared project vision.
- Defining a value-based delivery strategy.
- Generating solution options.
- Defining the business case.
- Project delivery – evaluating deliveries and driving regular reviews.

Situations where someone else wants to get something done are the trickiest to handle. These situations often arise when your boss calls you in and tells you that there is an important IT project and that you are going to represent him or her. You have been volunteered to be 'involved' in the project as the 'business representative' or some formal project title such as 'senior user'. You may not be very enthusiastic about the project or you may even think that it is a bad idea. Let's look at your options.

If you are not keen, you can say, as diplomatically as possible, that you don't want to be involved. This is rarely politic in most organisations in which I have worked, but it might be in some more enlightened companies. If you participate half-heartedly, it will be an uncomfortable experience. The project will go badly, you will have a miserable time and quite possibly you will get blamed for the project's failure. This doesn't sound like a great option.

Alternatively, you can reframe the way you look at the project and use it as a vehicle to explore the ideas in this book. Understand what your boss and other stakeholders see as the project's value. Get your boss' buy-in to value-based delivery and tell him or her about the key touchpoints. Explain that you need decision-making authority to get the value he or she wants. Assume the role of sponsor and go through the process of defining the vision, generating options and defining the business case. At this point you will either have an understanding of the value that the project brings to your organisation, and perhaps will become more enthusiastic, or your initial doubts may be proven to be justified.

If the former is the case, then go on to demonstrate how IT projects should be run and cover yourself in glory; if the latter is the case, then you have a real problem. You have been through a process that demonstrates that the project doesn't add value to the organisation but your boss still wants to do it. This situation does happen. The best advice I can give you to help you stay sane and survive is to read Chapters 4 and 7 and ensure that the project, at least, can be delivered in chunks, to lower risk. Or, maybe it is time to reconsider what sort of boss and organisation you want to work for?

The other option is that you might be genuinely enthusiastic about the project and mean it when you said 'thanks, it's a great opportunity, I will not let you down'. If that is the case, then the game-plan is exactly the same as if you were reluctant. Ask for buy-in to a delivery-based strategy and ask for the authority to make it work.

The third category of involvement that I listed at the start of this section was that you are going to be affected by the change, as a victim or beneficiary of the project, and you want to keep a watchful eye on it. In these circumstances, the key question is does the project have an effective sponsor? If the answer is no, then your challenge is either to find ways to fill the gap yourself by stealth or to offer to take on sponsorship responsibilities.

A canny friend of mine, who was an operations manager in a retail bank, found himself in this situation. He had a huge department that was going to be fundamentally affected by an IT project. He became concerned when the designated project sponsor did not show up at the project kick-off meeting or the subsequent progress report meetings. 'You have a lot on your plate', he said to the official sponsor, 'and this project affects my people more than anyone else. Why don't I take on the boring role of sponsor and we call you the project owner? You will still own the project but no one will bug you about the tiny details. You'll be like the chairman of the project!' The designated sponsor loved the idea and so the owner-sponsor model was born and it worked well.

KICKING AN INEFFECTIVE SPONSOR UPSTAIRS

Companies are run by their CEOs. When their time is done, they are often 'kicked upstairs' into the role of Chairman to ensure that their invaluable expertise and influence is not lost. Their role becomes less doing and more advisory, though they are usually consulted on the big decisions.

A sponsor should be like the CEO of a project. If you have an ineffective sponsor, you can consider inventing a chairman-type role, named something like 'project owner', and install someone more effective, possibly yourself, in the sponsor role. And, just like the chairman, the owner is there to advise and wield influence.

Using this Book

I want to emphasise something I said in the Introduction, as I know a lot of you will have skipped it. You can use this book in one of two ways. You can use it as a description of an end-to-end process for business leadership of your project or you can dip in and pick out tools that are relevant to a specific challenge that you have. Each of the tools in the book is designed to work both on its own and as part of an overall process. Trying out a tool doesn't commit you to swallowing everything in the book. I encourage you to experiment and find out what works for your project. Here is what the process looks like overall. We will go through each element in the next three chapters.

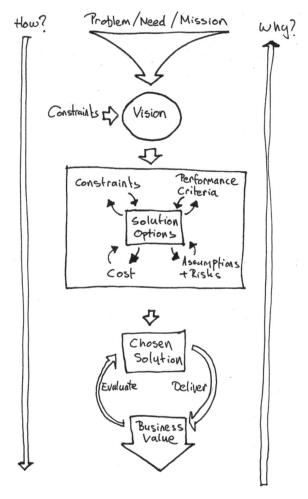

Figure 2.1   End-to-end process

How chapters address causes of project malfunction and frustrations of business managers	2. Stepping Up to the Plate	3. Defining a Shared Project Vision	4. Value-Based Delivery	5. Generating Solution Options	6. The Business Case ...	7. Project Delivery	8. Conclusion: A Team of Leaders
Causes							
Unclear business objectives		✓			✓		✓
Lack of senior management support	✓	✓	✓	✓	✓	✓	
Poor quality and changing requirements		✓	✓	✓		✓	✓
Lack of user involvement	✓	✓	✓	✓		✓	✓
Poor planning & risk management			✓	✓	✓	✓	✓
Frustrations							
Benefits not realised		✓	✓	✓	✓	✓	
Cost and time overrun			✓	✓		✓	
Lack of can-do attitude from IT		✓	✓	✓		✓	✓
Requirements/Solution mismatch		✓	✓	✓	✓	✓	
Inflexibility from IT		✓	✓	✓		✓	✓

Figure 2.2   Mapping of chapters to reasons for failure and frustrations

The matrix above, in Figure 2.2, sets out how each chapter impacts those causes and frustrations listed at the start of the chapter. A tick in a box in the matrix doesn't mean that the advice or tools in a particular chapter will solve the cause or frustration on its own; it means that it will make a significant contribution to addressing it. My aim, however, is to ensure that there are at least two against each problem in order to fully address it.

You don't have to read the whole of this book to get useful advice. Nor do you need to read the chapters sequentially. The book has been organised along a typical project life-cycle, so that you can quickly find advice that is relevant to where your project is right now. But whatever stage you are at, try to find an hour to flip through the early parts of the book. The seeds of project success or failure are usually sown in its early stages.

For the very busy, here are the most important pieces of advice contained in the book:

- *Don't do IT*: IT projects are expensive and risky. Don't embark on an IT project as a first resort. Make a genuine effort to identify alternative ways of realising your business outcomes, such as changing processes or buying a service that already exists.

- *Step up to the plate and take responsibility*: Don't be a hopeful spectator. It is up to you take leadership and to ensure that you get value. Don't stand on the sidelines and hope that everything will turn out fine.

- *Create a shared project vision of the project outcome*: Develop a rich picture, created together with key stakeholders who buy into it. Use the vision as a basis for solution generation and for guiding the actions of the project team during project delivery.

- *Insist on value-based delivery*: Structure the solution and project so that it delivers regular chunks of value that can be evaluated against performance criteria, assumptions costs and schedules.

- *Generate genuine solution options*: Set budget and schedule constraints up-front, together with quantified business performance criteria and other business constraints. Create a value profile for each option, including key assumptions, risks and cost.

- *Create a one or two-page business case summary*: Use the business case as a touchstone throughout the project and as the basis for regular reviews, rather than as something that is filed and forgotten about at the start of the project.

- *Take a proactive role during project delivery*: Evaluate value delivery against performance criteria, assumptions costs and schedules. Establish and chair regular meetings to review progress versus the business case. Review expenditure and progress versus the budget and schedule using earned value analysis. Review all key risks regularly and ensure that the project team is addressing risks and issues at least weekly.

Key Points from this Chapter

- The most common cause of IT project 'failure' is poor business leadership.

- The project sponsor has to step up to the plate and take responsibility for the project outcome.

- If the project sponsor does not have sufficient time to devote to leading the project, it is better to delegate authority to someone else who can.

- If an active sponsor is relatively junior, consider having someone more senior as project owner – sponsor and owner = CEO and Chairman.

- You can use this book as an overall guide or as a source of individual tools to try out.

3

Defining a Shared Project Vision

In this chapter I will talk about the power of a shared project vision and will suggest some tools to help you define a vision for your own project. I will use some well-known examples to illustrate the key points and to see what can be learned from real-world situations.

Doing the Right Project

Projects are created to change something. They solve a problem, fulfil a need or contribute towards a mission. For the purposes of this book, the terms 'problem', 'need' and 'mission' are interchangeable in terms of the role they play. They are what caused the project to be born. Often, they are slightly different ways of stating the same thing:

- Problem: lack of clean drinking water is a major cause of death in developing nations.

- Need: clean drinking water for families living on less than $1 to $2 per day.

- Mission: reduce by half the proportion of people without sustainable access to safe drinking water.

Missions or needs can often be reworded as problems, or vice versa. Some people are dogmatic and insist on asking 'so what's the problem statement?'. Initially, I prefer to stick with the way it was originally articulated because this is how the originators relate to it. Thus, if it is stated as a problem, then I take that as the start point. If it is stated as a need or mission, then I use that. What is key, however, is that the problem, need or mission is sufficiently well defined to ensure that the project will achieve the desired outcome. There is no point in doing the wrong project really well.

THE FIVE WHYS

The five whys is a useful way of checking whether you are addressing the cause or effect of a problem. It can equally be applied to needs and missions. It originated as a problem-solving technique used in the Toyota Production System that changed the face of car manufacturing.[1] The idea is simple: one asks 'why' up to five times to obtain the core reason for something.

For example:

1. Why are we doing this project?
   - So that we can scan paper insurance claim forms quickly.
2. Why do we want to scan insurance claims forms?
   - So that they are available to call centre agents.
3. Why do they need to be available to call centre agents?
   - Because customers often dispute the details.
4. Why do customers often dispute the details?
   - Because errors are made when keying them in.
5. Why are mistakes made when they are keyed in?
   - Because a lot of customer handwriting is difficult to read.

We have gotten to the root of the problem. Our project seems designed to enable us to win arguments with customers rather than solve the real problem.

In this instance, the first two whys were about what was presented as a need. It was only after the third question that we found a problem articulated. Although the technique is called the five whys, you can use alternative questions that have the same effect. I prefer to ask 'what would that give you?', which feels less brutal than asking why a few times in a row. But whatever question you use, it's best to ask the person or group you will be using it on for permission to do this exercise rather than just launch into it.

Identifying Constraints

The drinking water example, used at the start of this chapter, is based on a real project.[2] It was initiated by EWV, a division of Relief International, whose mission is to raise the living standards in developing countries by increasing access to technology and providing entrepreneurial opportunities for local people. Starting with the project's goal and asking why five times would end up trying to solve world poverty, which is a big ask. So what EWV effectively did was to make solution choices early on that act as constraints on the project's future solution choices.

Dirty water and poor sanitation cause 1.5 million deaths per year,[3] so EWV decided to constrain the project to that topic. This is still a huge problem to solve, so it decided to further constrain the project to drinking water. After reviewing previous drinking water initiatives, it constrained the solution further to rainwater harvesting. And finally, because of its mission, it constrained the problem further by saying that it had to be possible for the solution to be manufactured by local entrepreneurs. So we end up with a vision that says something like:

> *Households that are self-sufficient in safe drinking water, harvested from rain water, stored close by, avoiding the need to travel long distances, using collection and storage devices that can be manufactured and sold by local entrepreneurs.*

There are quite a few constraints in the vision, but there is still a very wide range of solution choices possible to achieve the vision. Ideally, a vision should have as few constraints as possible, but, as this example illustrates, projects often have to be bounded by constraints to keep their outcomes realistic. As we move through projects, from problem/need/mission towards a vision and then into specific solutions, more constraints will be imposed. Asking 'how?' moves us towards a solution and asking 'why?' takes us back towards the reason for the project.

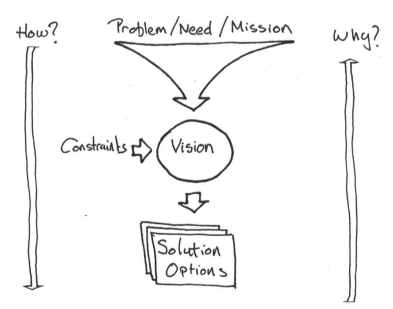

Figure 3.1   Vision to solution options

There is nothing wrong with having a vision that contains constraints as long as the choices to impose them are consciously made and the reasons are clear. I suggest that you keep a written list of constraints to ensure that they are visible and can be revisited if circumstances change. The key constraints should be listed in the business case summary described in Chapter 6.

Defining a Shared Vision

A shared vision brings your project's outcome to life. It describes what the world will be like after the project has been delivered. It describe the benefits that people will see, hear and feel. The more that it goes beyond a static picture and engages senses and emotions, the more memorable and compelling it will be. A good vision acts as the true north for your project team. It:

- describes the outcome that the project is seeking to achieve;

- engages customers and stakeholders in its creation and delivery;

- acts as a basis for generating alternative solutions;

- guides the actions of the project throughout the project.

Engaging the senses might seem like a stretch if your project is relatively straightforward, but there are some tools you can use to do just that. Rather than articulating explicitly how the senses are engaged, you can use the mind's power to enlist them by using familiar communication media. Here are some of the tools you can use to get your customers and stakeholders to collaborate together on a shared vision. Note that writing and drawing things out visibly, on say a flipchart, engages different areas of the brain to a solely verbal discussion, so it is well worth doing this element for the exercises below.

BRINGING THE VISION TO LIFE

The Movie Poster

Ask the key stakeholders to work together to draw a movie-style poster advertising the new service. What is the main image on the poster? What is the one sentence that sums it up? Who are main characters that are shown? What are the quotes from the critics? What emotions do you aim to evoke?

The Cover Story

This is a similar idea to the movie poster, except that the output is the cover of a popular tabloid newspaper, with punchy headlines, subheadings and quotes.[4] As before, think about the characters and the sort and the emotions aroused.

Design the Box

In this variation, the stakeholders work together to define the packaging for a box that describes the new service, with appropriate graphics, a description of the benefits and quotes from happy customers.[5]

TV Advert or Movie Trailer

I have used this to good effect in tandem with the movie poster. The team started by drawing the movie poster on a flip-chart and then moved on to storyboard the movie trailer, including suggested soundtrack.

Sometimes a vision appears to come fully formed from a single person. More usually, one finds that there has been a gestation period, during which the individual with the vision has been talking to a wide range of people, adapting and developing it as he or she goes.

THE SONY WALKMAN[6]

In 1978 Sony introduced a new stereo audio cassette recorder and player, the TC-D5. Masaru Ibuka, Sony's 70-year-old co-founder and Honorary Chairman, used to like to take one on flights in order to be able to listen to music. But at 1.7 kg (or 3.75 lb) it was a lot to carry around.

One day, before a trip to the USA, Ibuka asked Norio Ohga, the Deputy President, to create for him a simple, playback-only stereo version of *The Pressman*, the small, mono tape recorder that Sony had also launched in 1978. He was sufficiently impressed with the resulting player to show it to his co-founder and then Sony Chairman, Akio Morita: 'Try this. Don't you think a stereo cassette player that you can listen to while walking around is a good idea?' Morita agreed and in February 1979 Morita called a meeting at Sony Headquarters.

The group of predominantly young, electrical and mechanical design engineers, planners and publicity people were more than a little apprehensive, as well as curious, to hear why they had been summoned by the Chairman. Morita held up the modified Pressman and said:

> This is the product that will satisfy those young people who want to listen to music all day. They'll take it everywhere with them, and they won't care about record

> *functions. If we put a playback-only headphone stereo like this on the market, it'll be a hit. Our target market is students and other young people. We must launch it before the summer vacation at a price similar to the Pressman, which means less than 40,000 yen [40,000 yen was nearly £300. The TC-D5 was 100,000 yen or £750].*

In setting out the vision directly to the development team, Ibuka accomplished two things: first, his personal involvement conveyed the importance of the project; and, second, he ensured that the vision was not filtered or misheard.

The vision also defines the target market and sets two constraints, first for price and second for the timescale. This design to cost approach was common in Japanese manufacturing as it sought to capture foreign markets. It is a lesson that many IT projects would do well to learn from and a topic that I will return to in Chapter 5.

Something else to note about the Sony Walkman vision is that although it is not, at first glance, a very rich picture of the future state, it contains sufficiently familiar ideas to fuel the mind's power of association and to paint its own pictures. The picture is of happy, young people on the move under summer skies, listening to music on a lightweight device. A vision doesn't have to be long on detail to conjure up powerful moving images.

In his book *Thinking Fast and* Slow,[7] psychologist Daniel Kahneman explains that when reading something like the Walkman vision, the brain's 'associative machine' instantly draws on a wide range of associations, most of them unconscious. What happens in our heads is more like a movie trailer than a static picture or dead words on the page. The Walkman vision may be brief, but it fires up a rich picture.

Engaging with Customers and Stakeholders

While personal visions are common for entrepreneurially driven projects, many projects originate as a collective desire to solve a problem, to satisfy a need or to achieve a mission. The most powerful visions for these types of project are shared visions created collaboratively with customers and stakeholders. Management thinker Peter Senge sums this up well in his book *The Fifth Discipline*:

A vision is truly shared when you and I have a similar picture and are committed to one another having it, not just each of us, individually, having it. When people truly share a vision they are connected, bound together by a common aspiration.[8]

But even if the vision is a personal one, as the Sony Walkman example illustrates, it is still necessary to engage stakeholders within the organisation, including the development team, in order to gain support for and to deliver the vision.

I think most people are familiar with the concept of stakeholders, but in case any are not, here is my definition. A stakeholder is a person, group of people or an organisation that can affect or be affected by a project. It is sometimes beneficial to extend this definition to inanimate things such as regulation and legislation. Stakeholders may be within your own organisation or outside of it. Customers are clearly stakeholders, but I usually list them separately because they often get left out when it comes to active shaping activities.

Engaging customers and stakeholders from the beginning of the project provides it with a firm foundation for success. Project teams are often fearful of a dialogue with customers at these early stages, preferring to rely on surveys and focus groups. This is a form of engagement, but is not as powerful as sitting in with the project team and other stakeholders to help define the vision.

Some argue that if the project is going to launch a new product or service that is truly innovative, one should not consult customers, as they will be unable to relate it to their current experience. Henry Ford is alleged to have said that if he had asked customers what they wanted, they would have said faster horses. Most projects are not, however, as innovative as the first mass-produced motor car. And, at least one project that launched a truly revolutionary project was built on a foundation of consulting widely with both customers and stakeholders.

M-PESA[9]

Nick Hughes joined Vodafone in 2001. Part of his role was to help Vodafone understand how it could contribute to the United Nations's Millennium Development Goals initiative. That initiative aimed to encourage large commercial organisation's to help improve the lives of people in the developing world. In his role at Vodafone, Nick was already was aware that access to finance for the 'unbanked' was a major obstacle to development but hadn't, hitherto, had an opportunity to do anything about it.

In 2003 he was approached by a UK government department that offered to help part-fund a project that addressed Millennium Development Goals. The project would need to be commercially attractive to Vodafone, but Nick knew that the government funding would help to overcome internal hurdles. The terms of the government funding were that the project would need to involve the development of a product or service that was not previously available.

The first step was to convince the company to support and participate in a project. Nick says:

I spent a few weeks in mid-2003 putting together a proposal, whilst focusing on two things: broad support for the concept from a couple of very senior executives in the company, and the buy-in of my colleagues on the ground in East Africa. Both were fundamental to progress.

We set about organising a series of open workshops in Nairobi and Dar es Salaam. Invitees included banks, micro-finance organisations, other technology services suppliers, nongovernmental organisations with an interest in micro-credit, and representatives from the telecoms and finance sector regulators. We asked a question: Assume that the technology can do anything you want it to; what are the biggest challenges you face in growing your business or increasing access to financial services?

Out of the workshops, a pilot partnership was created between us (the network operators), a micro-finance institute (MFI), and a commercial bank. The view was that each could bring to the project a different set of competencies.

The proposition started to firm up around the design and test of a platform that would allow a customer to receive and repay a small loan using his or her [mobile phone]. We wanted to allow the customer to make payments as conveniently and simply as they do when they buy an airtime top-up, so a central feature of our proposition was to use the distribution network of Safaricom airtime resellers (or Agents in M-PESA terms) to facilitate this process. This service should also bring business efficiencies for the MFI and allow it to grow its business more quickly and to more remote locations than is possible using traditional paper processes.

The last paragraph of the above quote effectively describes the M-PESA vision. As we saw with the drinking water example, the vision already contains some solution choices that act as constraints:

- Customers receive and pay small loans with a mobile telephone.

- Using the distribution network of Safaricom airtime resellers.

It is arguable that if one removes these constraints, it opens up the possibility of alternative, perhaps better, solutions. This is fair comment, but a large number of diverse stakeholders have helped to develop this vision and it is a realistic example. Discussions with customers and stakeholders often result in a vision that has an element of solution and hence constraint.

M-PESA has been very successful in Kenya where it was launched. The ongoing support of customers and stakeholders was critical in making the vision a reality. At the end of 2010, the BBC website reported that 50 per cent of the Kenyan adult population was using M-PESA. It was subsequently launched in Tanzania, where it already has nine million subscribers, and more recently in South Africa and India.

The M-PESA story illustrates how important is was to engage stakeholders to get a project off the ground, to define the need, to co-create the vision and to help make that vision a reality.

Managing Stakeholders

In this section, I want to give you some tools to help you identify and manage the project stakeholders. The table below contains a set of questions that you can use to identify potential stakeholders. You can use it as a starting point, but I suggest that you work with your team to add to the list in the table and create a set of questions that are meaningful for your project and context. And once you have identified an initial list of stakeholders, you can ask those initial stakeholders who they would identify as additional stakeholders.

Table 3.1   Questions to identify potential stakeholders

Internal stakeholders	Who is affected by business process change? How will business and financial operations change? How will the organisation change? How will roles, responsibilities and rewards change? How will physical things such as buildings be affected? How will technology be affected? Whose help do we need to deliver it?
External stakeholders	How will customers be affected? How will suppliers/partners/the supply chain be affected? What regulations and laws do we need to consider? How will people and communities will be affected? How will creditors and shareholders be affected? How will representative bodies be affected? Who are the key influencers in our industry and media? How are our competitors affected? How is the environment affected?

Having identified the stakeholders, it is important to understand their attitude to the project. Are they supporters, opponents or indifferent? Having established their current attitude to the project, you need to determine what their attitude needs to be for the project to succeed. This will depend on their level of interest in the project and their power to affect it.

You don't need every stakeholder to be a supporter; influencing an opponent to be, and remain, indifferent can be a good result. Or perhaps you may need the active support of someone who is currently indifferent. And you must not be complacent with regard to supporters. Their attitude could change if you don't engage with them effectively throughout the life of the project.

You can start the process of stakeholder management during the identification brainstorm. As each stakeholder is identified, ask brainstorm participants to write the stakeholder name on different-coloured Post-it notes:

- green if you think they will support the project;

- red if you think they will oppose or hinder the project;

- yellow if you are not sure;

- blue if you think they will be indifferent.

Then ask participants to attach the Post-its to a flip-chart with two axes that describe the relative power and interest of the stakeholders, as shown in Figure 3.2.

This mapping of stakeholders provides a good visual basis for managing stakeholders and helps identify where best to target your effort in doing so. For example, it should be pretty clear that if you have someone on a red Post-it note who has a high degree of both power and interest, then you need to invest time to engage with him or her. If, however, someone is on a blue Post-it note who has a low degree of both power and interest, it is pretty safe to ignore him or her.

Don't forget that there may well be 'reds' and 'yellows' in the room when you are doing the brainstorm. If there are, you need to demonstrate that you genuinely want to understand their concerns and that you are serious about addressing them.

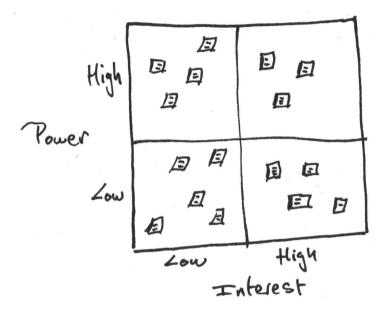

Figure 3.2   Stakeholder mapping

Having done this initial mapping, you need to validate your initial colour guesses through conversations with the stakeholders that you have identified. A good way of doing this is to work with stakeholders to understand what value they get from the status quo and how the realisation of the project vision will change that. Ask whether a given stakeholder, for example, gain or lose value if the vision is achieved?

Arne van Oosterom, founder of DesignThinkers Group, introduced me to the idea of mapping value flows between stakeholders in order to bring the idea of stakeholder value to life. On the following page is an illustration of what the existing value flows might look like for a project that aims to help homeless people (see Figure 3.3 on the next page). This diagram can be developed, together with stakeholders, to be used a basis for understanding how the value flows would change after the successful delivery of a particular vision or solution option.

The diagram illustrates that there are many different types of value. Here are some types of value that you can think about when you draw a value flow diagram:

- Money.

- Love.

- Power.

- Attention.

- Information.

- Trust.

- Reputation.

- Expenses.

- Rights.

- Service.

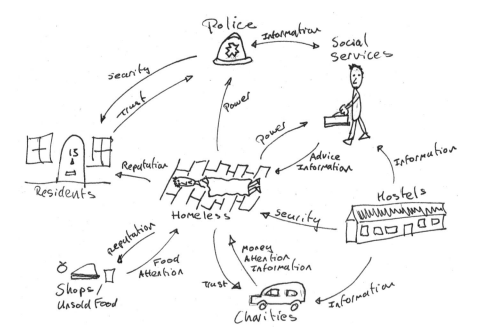

Figure 3.3   Example of stakeholder value flow

- Credits.

- Product exposure.

- Security.

- Control.

WHAT IS VALUE?

I have deliberately chosen the term 'value' rather than 'benefit' because value conveys a combination of both benefit and cost – or, to coin a phrase, it is the bang for the buck.

Value is, however, in the eye of its beholders. If the only benefit conveyed by buying a Rolex is the ability to tell the time accurately, few would be sold. It is important, therefore, to engage with stakeholders to understand how they perceive value.

Value flow diagrams are also useful tools when thinking about stakeholder emotions and needs. I have already talked about engaging emotions for the project vision, but it may still feel a little odd to talk about emotions in the context of IT projects. However, behaviour and decisions are often based on emotion rather than logic, something that projects should take into account.

For example, when British Airways opened Terminal 5 at Heathrow Airport, customers were confronted by a battery of automated check-in machines rather than desks staffed by service agents. Presumably, the project vision was to have automated self-service that sped happy customers through a fast, reliable and easy check-in experience, reducing errors and delays, and at the same time saving money through reduced staff costs and enhancing British Airways' image as a modern innovative company.

I was an early visitor to the new terminal and watched the behaviour of customers. There were long queues at the few staffed check-in desks, while most of the machines stood unused. Customers would approach the machines and hover at a slight distance, trying to evaluate the difficulty of use, fearing that closer inspection might commit them to action and possible embarrassment.

British Airways had anticipated the problem of novelty by having staff on hand to assist. Unfortunately, however, many customers, fearing the embarrassment of looking foolish, made a run for it when staff approached. Some customers got frustrated with the new machines and vented their anger at staff. And a reasonable proportion of customers used the machines without problem and walked away smiling, enjoying their own cleverness at figuring out how to use the machine and speed past the queues. There were a lot of emotions on show, not least for staff, and it was clear that the project's probability of realising its value could be increased by understanding and addressing those emotions.

The Job is Not Done When the Ship Sails

I want to conclude with a well-known example: the Apple iPhone. This reinforces a number of points that have already been discussed, but also highlights the importance of leadership throughout the life of a project.

THE IPHONE

Bob Borchers, former iPhone product marketing engineer, gave a talk to students at a California school in which he described how the iPhone came into being:

'What's interesting is that the challenge Steve [Jobs] laid out for us when we created the iPhone wasn't to make a touch-screen device that would play apps and do all of this stuff', Borchers told students. 'His [charge] was simple. He wanted to create the first phone that people would fall in love with. That's what he told us'.

'Now if you're an engineer, like I am by training, you're like "what the heck does that mean?"', he said. 'But he was right. The idea was, he wanted to create something that was so instrumental and integrated in peoples' lives that you'd rather leave your wallet at home than your iPhone'.

'The product had to be a revolutionary mobile phone, the best iPod to date, and also let users carry "the internet in their pocket," the latter of which was somewhat of a foreign concept at the time', Borchers said. Downloadable apps, advanced GPS capabilities, video and photography features, and voice integration weren't part of the original mandate.

Instead, those features blossomed from Apple's successful formation of a platform that could continue to surprise and delight users over time, with Jobs in particular exercising his penchant for perfection and attention to detail every step of the way.[10]

I think it's reasonable to describe 'create the first phone that people would fall in love with' as a mission. Jobs doesn't begin with must-have functionality, as most might; he leads with the most powerful and universal emotion that there is. Perhaps only someone like Jobs would have the credibility to use the word 'love' without it sounding ludicrous.

That it was to be a 'phone' imposes an immediate constraint on the solution design. It may sound perverse to describe it as a constraint, but if one goes up a level of abstraction by asking 'why a phone?', then one gets to the *need* to communicate on the go. For example, Jobs could have said something like:

> *I want people anywhere in the world to be able to communicate instantly with other people and access the Internet in a way that they will love.*

Remember that Google asked its top engineers to reinvent online communication and collaboration, without being constrained by it having to be email, instant messaging, forums or groups. It wanted to throw away the 'how' and rethink the solution. The result was Google Wave. A lot of early adopters thought that Google Wave was very cool, but Google finally concluded that email was too deeply embedded to get people to change. After failing to get sufficient traction, Google decided to ditch its innovative offspring.

But Apple's success was based on creating beautifully designed solutions that combined pre-existing technologies in novel ways for products such as the iPod. One has to guess that Jobs took account of how deeply phones had become embedded in our lives and culture, so the constraint on the product being a phone made perfect sense.

It's not clear whether it was Jobs or the team who added the phrase 'the internet in their pocket' to the iPhone vision, but it is crucial in bringing the vision to life. The reference to being the best iPod to date is also interesting because at that time the iPod used a navigation wheel, not a touch-screen. It illustrates that although the designers were constrained to it being a phone, the vision was sufficiently unconstrained to allow them to ditch an already innovative design in order to achieve their goal. In any event, the iPhone vision essentially distils down to:

> *The first phone that people would fall in love with. Something so instrumental and integrated in peoples' lives that you'd rather leave your wallet at home than your iPhone. A revolutionary mobile phone, the best iPod to date that lets users carry the internet in their pocket.*

Like the Sony Walkman, the vision doesn't need to be described in great detail. There are enough associations for our minds to generate rich pictures of how it would be used.

I want to highlight that the report of Borchers's talk concludes by saying the project proceeded 'with Jobs in particular exercising his penchant for perfection and attention to detail every step of the way'. As anyone who has read Jobs' biography[11] will know, this is close to understatement. Although he had given the team a lot of latitude, he was intimately involved in the project as it progressed.

LEADERSHIP DOESN'T STOP WITH SETTING THE VISION

It isn't enough for you to define a clear vision and assume that it will be realised. Pointing a sailing boat at New York as it leaves England is not enough to ensure that it arrives in the right place. A project's journey is rarely a straight line. Success depends on constantly checking and adjusting course in order to arrive at the desired destination.

Key Points from this Chapter

- A shared vision is a rich picture of the project outcome that engages as many senses and emotions as possible.

- You want to ensure that the project addresses the right problem, need or mission.

- Visions should be mainly about what needs to be achieved, not how.

- Realistically, visions are likely to contain some element of solution which acts as a constraint on possible solution options.

- Engaging with and managing stakeholders throughout the project is critical to success.

- The job of leadership isn't done once the ship sets sail.

WHAT IF YOUR PROJECT IS ALREADY WELL UNDER WAY?

It is never too late to define or check your vision; it's only too late when you have run out of money.

If you don't have a clearly articulated vision, you will find that your stakeholders and development team will welcome an exercise to make it explicit. There may or may not be misalignment. Either way, you need to check that you are spending money to reach the right destination.

Similarly, if your project already has a vision, check it against the criteria set out in this chapter and ask whether it is clear and whether everyone on the project understands it. Even if you wrote it by following the guidelines in this chapter, I suggest that you revisit your vision with stakeholders and your team on a regular basis, as suggested in Chapter 6. Memories are poor and projects drift off-course gradually.

Don't be afraid to ask the toughest question: do we still want this project? Getting projects started can be hard, but stopping them can be even harder. Avoid pouring good money after bad.

4

Value-Based Delivery

The central message of this chapter is that your project should adopt a strategy that delivers *regular value* to customers and stakeholders throughout the project. Don't accept a strategy which requires you to wait until the end of the project to get all of the value. Making this clear to your team and your suppliers at the start of the project enables them to create and design a solution that is structured for regular value delivery.

In addition to early value delivery, your strategy should enable you to evaluate regularly:

- the *value* delivered versus expectations;

- the actual *cost* compared to the forecast;

- the actual *duration* compared to the forecast;

- the actual *solution* delivered versus what you thought you would get;

- the *quality* of what was delivered.

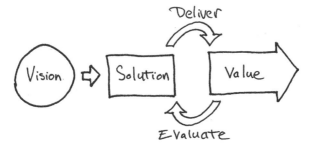

Figure 4.1 **Regular value delivery**

The delivery of each increment of the project's overall value provides an opportunity for the project team to learn and adjust course, rather than wait until the end of the journey and discover that the project has arrived at the wrong place.

Let me use an example from the house renovation television programme *Grand Designs* to illustrate what I mean by regular value delivery and its associated benefits.

A Grand Design

The following scenario will be familiar to regular watchers of the programme.

It's January. An enthusiastic couple are pictured outside a huge but dilapidated building that they intend to renovate in an architecturally novel way. They describe their vision for their 'grand design'. They tell us that it will be the family home of their dreams.

We are told that they sold their previous home and sank all of their money into this project which will realise their grand design. They will live in temporary, very basic, accommodation adjacent to where the work will be taking place. Their budget is £800,000 and they aim to be in their new home just in time for Christmas. They are confident that the budget and timescale is realistic.

Fast forward to December. An unhappy and bickering couple are standing in the snow, in front of a huge, eight-bedroomed property with no roof on it. The project is running behind schedule, it is way over budget and they have run out of money. They have no idea where they are going to get the money to finish the project.

Why Do Grand Designs Overrun?

The people whose dream homes are featured on *Grand Designs* usually have a clear shared vision of what they want, so this is not usually the cause of the problem, as is often the case with IT projects. Also, the participants in *Grand Designs* definitely view themselves as customers (and I shall refer to them as such throughout the discussion here) and their proximity and involvement in the project means that they will be on hand throughout to make decisions about details when required.

Unfortunately, both builders and customers get blown off-course by the novelty of their projects and their innate bias towards optimism.[1] Unless we have done something before, we can only guess at how long it will take or cost. This is true of any 'project', from going on a hike to putting someone on Mars. If we have done something hundreds of times before, we can make an accurate estimate of how long it will take or cost the next time that we can do it. If we have done it a few times before, we can make an educated guess. If we have never done it before, we can only make a pure guess; the greater the novelty of the project *to us* and our team, the less accurate the estimate. Other people's experience can inform our guess, but their capability and context may have been very different when looked at closely. In addition, they may simply have gotten lucky with their outcome.

In *Grand Designs* the problem of novelty manifests itself in a couple of ways. First, the unexpected occurs and, second, there is the need to make regular decisions about details. The unexpected can be anything from a protected species of bats nesting in the roof of an old barn to an ancient water well under the site that is causing rising damp.

The decisions on details are usually things that haven't previously been considered fully. For example, the builder might ask the couple how they want to light the bedrooms. Invariably, they want the best possible solution

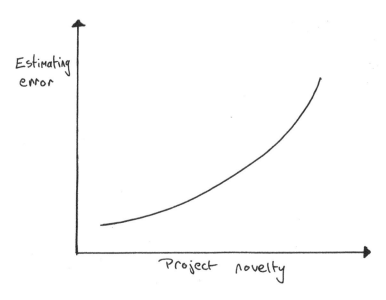

Figure 4.2   Project novelty versus estimating error

and end up going for the most expensive option. The cost difference between the options involved in each of these decisions does not seem great, but they mount up, accumulating into a big number. In addition, decisions made in haste in order to avoid delay can later turn out to have been ill-informed and costly in the long run.

QUESTION: HOW DOES A PROJECT GET TO BE A YEAR LATE?

Answer: One day at a time.

(Fred Books, writing about software projects in *The Mythical Man-Month*)[2]

So what could be done differently?

Realising a Grand Design through Regular Value Delivery

If a project is novel to you and your builder (or IT supplier), you should both accept that any estimate is going to be a guess. Adopting a value-based approach ensures that you get value for the money that you spend, rather than taking an all-or-nothing approach. In addition, it allows you to refine the overall estimates of cost and duration, based on the performance of each value delivery increment.

For the *Grand Designs* project, I would recommend that the customers work with the builder and his team to create a strategy that delivers regular value. A close working relationship with the builder is paramount, so that the builder and his team share the vision and understand how the customer perceives value. When this is the case, the builder and his team are likely to contribute problem-solving ideas, at a macro- and micro-level, rather than mindlessly executing a plan and raising problems that are seen as being the customer's responsibility to solve.

With a good working relationship, the customers and the builder can work together to identify a sequence of value deliveries that take into account the benefit to cost trade-offs. Some builders would not want to adopt this type of approach and might argue that it will be cheaper and quicker if the customers simply define what they want, accurately and in advance of the project starting, and simply let the builder get on with it. This is a similar conversation to those I have often had with IT suppliers. Unfortunately, it is rarely possible to accurately define everything in advance, as we will discuss in the next section.

Builders (and IT suppliers) may also argue that it will be more expensive to engineer a solution that delivers incrementally. In my experience, this cost is usually exaggerated and can be minimised if it is clear from the beginning that the customer wants an incremental approach.

It is within the customers' power to choose a cooperative builder who, in this example, might help you to identify a sequence of value that looks like this:

- A flushing toilet, with privacy.

- Somewhere the family can wash and dry their hands.

- Somewhere to shower, with privacy.

- Somewhere to cook.

- A quiet bedroom for the children.

- A quiet bedroom for the parents.

- Somewhere with electricity to use a computer, play games and watch television.

- Other rooms in priority order.

Note that there is already some element of solution present in the definitions of value. It says 'a flushing toilet, with privacy' rather than 'somewhere private and hygienic to go to the toilet'. Possible solutions have been consciously constrained. Solutions could have been further constrained by defining the value required as a toilet within a bathroom, finished to the standard expected for the final property. Indeed, the customers could ask for the whole property to be delivered, room by room, to the standards expected on completion of the overall build. As each room is delivered, the customers would be able to evaluate whether:

- they received the value they expected;

- it cost more than the estimate and by how much;

- it took longer than the estimate and by how much;

- the overall 'solution' was consistent with expectations;

- the quality of the work met their expectations;

- the team understood and responded to their needs;

- the team gave them confidence that it could deliver the whole project;

- they enjoyed working with the team.

These benefits represent a type of value in themselves in the form of reduced project risk.

YOU STILL NEED AN OVERALL ESTIMATE FOR FORECASTING

Although you accept that the initial estimate for the project is unlikely to be accurate, you should still ask your supplier to provide their best estimate for each value delivery and hence the overall project.

The performance for each completed value delivery can then be factored into the estimates for future value deliveries for the project and consequently improve the accuracy of the overall forecast. The more deliveries the team has under its belt, the better the forecasts for the value deliveries and the overall project. This is actually truer in IT projects than it is in this building example.

This is because when an IT project adopts a regular value delivery strategy, it is largely the same the team that carries out design, build, test and implementation activities for each successive value delivery. And, broadly speaking, they will be using the same tools, in the same environment, with the same customer. It is therefore reasonable to use past productivity performance, within the project, as a good basis for forecasting future performance.

Another side-benefit benefit of completing the project room by room might be that different trades (such as carpentry, plumbing and electricity) are on site at the same time, working together and talking about how best to achieve a particular outcome. This could avoid costly rework at a later stage that might be caused by misunderstandings and unchecked assumptions. Fixing something that is already embedded in a finished product is expensive and often occurs in IT projects. Reducing the accumulation of small mistakes early in the project before they are embedded in the product can reduce the total cost considerably, going some way towards offsetting the cost of the incremental approach to value delivery.

The final benefit of the room-by-room approach is that if the customers run out of money, they will still have a home in which they can enjoy a comfortable Christmas. Some way into the project, they may even decide that they don't really need eight bedrooms after all and stop at four or six in order to stay within budget.

Of course, one doesn't have to take a room-by-room approach to accrue the benefits of regular evaluation. However, it does illustrate the importance of thinking about value, solution options and delivery strategy at the same time.

There are many parallels between a typical grand design and the problems usually associated with IT projects:

- The degree of novelty.

- The high probability of cost and schedule overrun.

- The high cost of changes when the project is at an advanced stage.

- Small changes accumulating into a significant cost.

- Having to wait until the end of the project to get value.

Nevertheless, IT projects have an additional characteristic that makes the case for regular value delivery even stronger. *Grand Designs* projects are created with physical products, whose definition is clearly understood and visualised in a common way by the customer and the supplier. For example, a wall, a bath, a door or a ceiling all have a consistent meaning; they are 'hardware'. If the customer wants a bathtub, everyone knows what it means and the customer can choose from a catalogue of options. It is a process of narrowing down from a range of easily visualised options.

In contrast, much of an IT project is created from non-physical products: 'software'. In the main, these products are not well defined and mutually understood. For example, a system for processing insurance claims or a website for ordering bespoke shirts are descriptions of need or function rather than the product, because the product is not well defined or understood.

As a consequence, IT projects usually spend considerable time trying to define what is required and what it will look like when it is delivered, usually referred to as 'requirements' and 'design', respectively. Getting a good 'specification' of requirements and design is one of the major challenges for IT projects.

The Waterfall Model

In the early 1980s, IT projects began to increase in scale and complexity. Practitioners looked to other industries in order to understand how to better manage large-scale, complex projects. The most obvious comparator seemed to be the large-scale construction of physical things such as skyscrapers, dams, bridges, oil rigs, power stations and so on, which followed a similar pattern:

- Figure out what is wanted – the 'requirements'.

- Design it.

- Build it.

- Test it.

- Implement it.

The idea is to complete each stage and 'get it right' before moving on to the next stage. Some clarification is allowed for in each successive stage, but the aim is to avoid the often considerable cost of rework associated with changing one's mind at a later stage. This approach was emulated by IT suppliers and became known as 'the waterfall model' (see Figure 4.3 opposite).

Unfortunately, this model doesn't work as well for IT as it does for construction. Construction is a much more mature industry, with documentation standards that are tied to well-defined physical outputs. IT practitioners responded to this by trying to introduce documentation standards that make IT projects more engineering-like. Sadly, the standards that have been developed are local, variable and non-binding. The continuing high failure rates of IT projects, as set out at the start of this book, seem to indicate that the efforts to emulate engineering have not had a great deal of positive impact. Indeed, a good proportion of IT practitioners now argue that such efforts are doomed to failure because software is not a clearly delineated physical output.

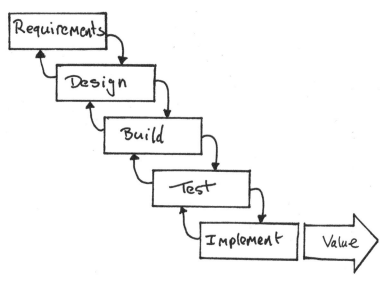

Figure 4.3   Waterfall life-cycle

The problem for IT projects begins with requirements. Any large project carries the risk that the supplier will not deliver what the customer hoped for or expected; the larger the project, the greater the need to reduce this risk. The waterfall model attempts to solve this by creating a written description of what the customer wants and what the supplier will deliver, so that the solution can be agreed in advance of the work taking place. Unfortunately, there is no industry-wide definition of what constitutes requirements. Indeed, much of what is usually described as requirements is actually a mixture of requirements and high-level design that describes how the requirements will be satisfied, rather than pure requirements described as business outcomes.

The result is a large amount of documentation that increases in proportion to the project size. The amount of documentation is bloated by the desire to capture everything in as much detail as possible, assuming that every eventuality can be foreseen. It is further bloated if the delivery date is far away in the future. This creates a desire to ensure that no requirements miss the bus, in turn causing the delivery date to disappear further into the future because the project has to deliver more.

The greater the amount of documentation, the greater the difficulty for those writing it to ensure that it is correct. And, correspondingly, the greater the difficulty for those reading it to comprehend and act on it as was intended by the authors. Throw in the lack of standardisation and the lack of well-defined outputs and there are lots of opportunities for misunderstandings.

In addition, changes to the requirements or design during the course of the project, in response to newly discovered or new business needs, become difficult. Changes to the documentation can introduce errors and have unforeseen consequences in related sections of the document. Voluminous documentation created to reduce risk becomes self-defeating.

And if all of that were not enough, many of the requirements will never be implemented, as they fall victim to trade-offs between cost, schedule and scope. They are relegated to 'the next phase', which never seems to happen. The cost of writing (and reviewing) these requirements is a waste. The Standish Group's 2010 *CHAOS Manifesto*[3] estimates that 'only about 20 per cent of [specified] features and functions specified ever get used'.

An Agile Approach

The drawbacks of the waterfall model prompted IT suppliers and thinkers to explore alternative approaches. In 1986, Barry Boehm, Chief Scientist at aerospace manufacturer TRW, proposed a 'spiral model' for software development.[4]

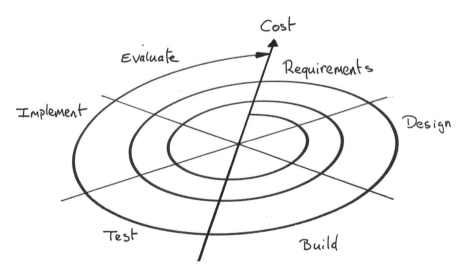

Figure 4.4   Spiral model

This was probably the first time that someone published a proposal for an iterative approach as an alternative to the waterfall. The goal of the spiral is to take a number of smaller bites out of the project outcome, regularly reviewing success and priorities, before deciding on the next steps.

Over the next 15 years, practitioners tried a range of iterative approaches, with the rationale that:

- it is futile to try to think of and document every requirement in advance;

- what is described as requirements is often design;

- requirements and design are best described in concert;

- the desire for exact definition leads to voluminous documentation that is difficult to review and susceptible to authoring and comprehension errors;

- seeing the solution come alive during design, build and test will lead to a reconsideration of the requirements and design;

- business requirements will develop and change during the project.

The iterative innovators realised that, when it comes to IT projects, software has a positive advantage over physical products. Approached with the right mindset, software can be created, reviewed and amended quickly. Rather than getting things perfectly specified in advance, one can 'fail', learn and adjust quickly. But Boehm's paper didn't exactly light the blue touch paper. The waterfall model continued to be the predominant model. Then in 2001, a group of influential IT practitioners and thinkers got together and wrote 'the Agile Manifesto'.[5]

Since then, 'agile' has been the term used to describe most iterative or incremental approaches. Agile approaches have gained a lot of ground. However, the very term 'agile' is polarising when one speaks to IT practitioners. A good proportion of practitioners are still sceptical about agile approaches and regard proponents as dangerous, deluded radicals. They argue that agile approaches are unworkable for large complex projects. They also argue, often with justification, that agile approaches are used as an excuse for getting on and building software without thinking it through properly. None of this is helped by the zealotry of some agile proponents, who see 'agile' as the only true way, with damnation guaranteed for everyone else.

A Value-Based Strategy

I have discussed waterfall and agile approaches because I believe it will help you if you understand where your IT supplier sits on the spectrum. It should be pretty obvious that regular value delivery is going to fit better with an agile approach than with a waterfall approach. However, because of the emotive nature of the term 'agile', I recommend that you simply insist on an approach that delivers regular value. If your supplier is an agile proponent, then this should be easy. However, if your supplier is a waterfall proponent, you might have to influence them to do a series of small waterfalls (as shown in Figure 4.5). This can work fine as long as they are structured for regular value delivery.

If you are using an external supplier, you may get pressure from within your own organisation to try to dissuade you from the strategy I have been advocating, for 'commercial reasons'. The pressure may come from a procurement department or internal IT management, who advise you to 'nail down the requirements' before asking an external supplier to quote a fixed price.

The tendency to adopt a fixed price approach, based on 'nailed-down requirements', seems to increase when software development is going to be done by an offshore supplier. The offshore option is usually adopted because the offshore work is done at much lower day rates. This causes managers to

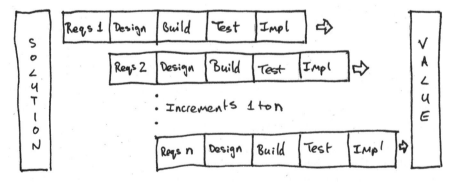

Figure 4.5　Regular value delivery with a series of waterfalls

think about the work as being divided into two parts: as the visible onshore stuff being performed by expensive people (the requirements) and the less visible offshore stuff being performed by inexpensive people (the software development). Having mentally divided the problem into these two parts, managers have already fallen into a waterfall mindset that separates requirements and development. In addition, there may be a belief that the offshore work is less in control because it is out of view and is therefore more prone to overrun.

However, in addition to the already-discussed drawbacks of a waterfall approach:

- if the supplier has quoted a fixed price for the 'nailed down' requirements, any changes provide the supplier with an opportunity to increase the price;

- you will be charged handsomely for changes. This accumulates and is expensive;

- if something in the requirements isn't clear, the supplier's people are more likely to make an assumption about what is meant and carry on without seeking clarification;

- it can be more difficult to get an early sight of what is being developed;

- you lose out on being able to harness the creativity of the development team.

It's not impossible to make a fixed-price waterfall approach work for IT projects, but it is very challenging. I would advise you not to go down this route and to avoid the inevitable charge of 'well, you signed it off' when the product delivered is not what you expected.

Validating Assumptions – A Particular Kind of Value

There is a particular type of value that should get priority as part of the delivery strategy. This value is the validation of key assumptions upon which the project business case depends; for example, the number of repeat purchases made by customers or the number of customers who continue with a service after a trial period ends. In the next chapter, I will describe an approach that generates solution options, where each option has a profile that includes key assumptions. (As you will see, these may also be expressed as risks, performance criteria or constraints.)

Validated business case assumptions have particularly high value. Your entire project depends on them being within a range of permissible error. A key objective of your delivery strategy, therefore, should be to validate key assumptions as early and as cost-effectively as possible. This may mean that you want a particular part of the solution delivered first in order to enable you to validate a key assumption. Or it may be that you want to build a prototype, with limited functionality, to validate the critical assumptions. Unless these needs are included up-front as part of your delivery strategy, they will get jettisoned as nice-to-haves later in the project when things start to get hectic.

In addition to business assumptions, there may be some key technical assumptions that you want to tease out. Is there is an untested technical assumption that could derail your project? If so, testing it early delivers business value. You don't have to get into the technical details, but it is worth asking your supplier whether there are any such assumptions upon which the overall technical solution is dependent, such as the use of a product that is new to their team. But take care if your supplier tells you there is a critical assumption that will take half the budget to validate – it's probably not the solution you want!

More Support for a Regular Value Delivery Strategy

In 'The Six Myths of Product Development', published in the *Harvard Business Review*,[6] Harvard Professor Stefan Thomke and consultancy president Donald Reinersten report on their experience across a range of industries, including semiconductors, cars, consumer electronics, medical devices, software and financial services. Essentially, they conclude that iterative approaches, structured for frequent learning, are more successful than waterfall-type approaches. 'Treat the development plan as a hypothesis that will evolve as new information becomes available' is one of their key recommendations.

Further support comes from a surprising quarter: the construction industry. Over the last 10 years, the concept of 'Lean Construction' has been getting increasing traction. The term 'lean' was popularised by the book

The Machine That Changed the World.[7] This book described the impact of 'the Toyota Production System' on the global car market. Construction projects are increasingly applying lean principles to their projects.

The authors of *The Machine That Changed the World* set out the 'five principles of lean thinking',[8] which are consistent with the delivery strategy that I have set out in this chapter:

1.   Identify customers and specify value.

2.   Identify and map the value stream.

3.   Create flow by eliminating waste.

4.   Respond to customer pull.

5.   Pursue perfection (where every asset and every action adds value for the end customer).

Finally, although my recommendation is that you don't tell your IT supplier how to do their job, it is worth knowing that the Standish Group's *CHAOS Manifesto, 2010*[9] reports that:

> *Software applications developed through the* agile process have three times the success rate *of the traditional waterfall method and a much lower percentage of time and cost overruns.*

Key Points from this Chapter

- Cost and schedule estimates for IT projects are often no more than guesses.

- Regular value delivery side-steps the estimating trap and delivers usable value.

- Creating voluminous detailed documentation to nail down requirements creates more, not less risk.

- What are termed requirements are often a form of design.

- Regular value delivery provides regular opportunities to evaluate cost and quality.

- Think agile, but don't say it out loud to your supplier.

- Validate key business and technical assumptions as early and cheaply as possible.

WHAT IF YOUR PROJECT IS ALREADY WELL UNDER WAY?

If your IT supplier is taking an agile approach, then simply change the focus from the regular delivery of functionality (or software) to one of regular delivery of value. To do this, you will need to work together with the supplier to explain where you get most benefit and combine this with cost of delivery in order to determine the best sequence of value.

If your IT supplier is taking a waterfall approach, you can still adjust. Work with your supplier to group requirements into different value increments. This should not be difficult to do, as the supplier will have already based cost estimates on the requirements, or the design if you have reached that stage. You can then have a discussion with your supplier about how to deliver these value increments as a series of mini-projects (or waterfalls) that give you regular value delivery.

Even if you are in the testing stage of a waterfall project, you can still identify value increments that can be tested and put into production, in sequence, without waiting for a big bang.

5

Generating Solution Options

The purpose of this chapter is to help you generate a range of genuinely different options, based on value, to deliver the project vision. If the vision describes *what* you want to achieve, a 'solution' describes, in business terms, *how* you will achieve it. It describes the role played by IT as part of the overall business solution, but it is not a technical specification of the IT component of the solution.

For example, take the project to help the homeless that was referred to in Chapter 3. Let's say that the mission is to use information technology to improve the lives of homeless people. Your vision might be to provide homeless people with information about things such as the availability of beds in hostels and shelters in their area, free food from food banks and food stores at closing time, medical services, drug and alcohol dependency services, employers who will take on homeless people, communication to family and so on.

One solution would be to provide homeless people with some form of mobile device. Another might be to install private kiosks with static devices in selected locations such as railway stations and hostels. The solution for a static device might be that it is to be touch-screen, multilingual and have a text-to-speech option for those who are illiterate. These are solution options that describe the role played by IT, but not the technical specification. It doesn't say whether a device is a PC or some other device. It doesn't talk about operating system or network connectivity. It describes the value or function that IT delivers, not how it is delivered.

The distinction is important because IT people often talk in terms of 'solutions' by which they usually mean how the solution is engineered, rather than what it delivers, or a mixture of both. As a business manager, you only need to be interested in the value delivered, not the technical engineering.

Generating Solutions is an Iterative Process

Thinking doesn't progress in a straight line. Let's say your vision is to spend a spring birthday weekend in Paris with someone you love, seeing the sights, visiting art galleries, eating in nice restaurants, shopping and soaking up the general ambience that is Paris in the springtime. A significant part of your 'solution' will be travel and accommodation.

However, unless you are a regular visitor, you are unlikely to jump straight to the solution. If you live in London, for example, you might compare the relative cost and convenience of travelling to Paris by train on Eurostar with the offerings of the various airlines that fly there. If the duration of your visit is limited, an early arrival time into the centre of Paris may have particular value for you. As you weigh up the options, you will be making value trade-offs, comparing the different bundles of benefits relative to their cost. Companies offering weekend breaks that include both travel and accommodation might be another attractive option?

If you've been through this sort of process, you will know that it's a process of iteration, trying out different combinations of costs and benefits, until you settle on the best solution for your vision.

IT projects should be no different. All too often, however, minds are made up in advance. A linear sequence of thought ends with a single solution that is favoured by the IT supplier. Then, because the customer's governance process requires more than one solution to be considered, two additional solutions are added and we get:

1.   the hugely expensive gold-plated solution;

2.   the solution that the supplier favours;

3.   the ludicrously sub-optimal solution.

You can avoid this solution cul-de-sac by adopting a process that deliberately uses a variety of viewpoints to slow down thinking and engage the logical parts of our brains.[1] For IT projects, I suggest that you use four different viewpoints. These different viewpoints will combine together to form different solutions, each with a different value profile. The viewpoints, or dimensions, that I recommend are:

1.   constraints;

2.   performance criteria;

3.   cost;

4.   assumptions;

5.   risks.

This process can work at a macro- or micro-level, for the overall solution and for components of the solution, respectively. Let's go back to our example of using technology to help homeless people and assume that we have decided to

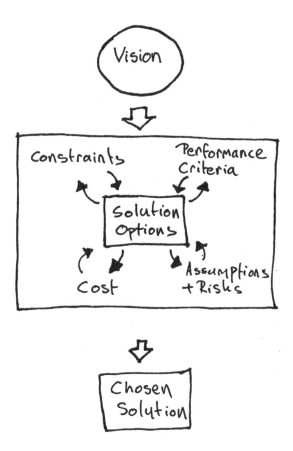

Figure 5.1   Vision to chosen solution option

locate kiosks at railway stations. In developing the solution to fulfil the vision, the discussion might go something like this:

- What is the budget?

- How many locations will it support?

- Would it be cheaper to use keyboards?

- How often would keyboards need to be replaced if they were stolen or broken?

- Do we want to limit the time spent in the kiosk? If so, how long should this be?

- Is touch-screen faster than keyboard?

- Would it be much cheaper to only use English?

There is continuous exploration of trade-off's across the four dimensions in order to arrive at a range of options. Each of these options should have a different profile across the four dimensions, to give you a genuine choice of alternatives.

SOLUTIONS SHOULD INCLUDE DATA NEEDED TO VALIDATE KEY ASSUMPTIONS

In order to validate key business case assumptions, you need to make clear what data you need to do so and ensure that the solution design incorporates production of that data. For example, you might want to see data that help you to understand customer buying behaviour or operator error rates. You cannot assume that the data you need will be a byproduct of the solution – *you need to ask for it*. Adding it as an afterthought could be expensive and too late to be useful.

Note, later in this chapter I will talk about key performance criteria whose measurement data also needs to be designed into the solution, not thought about afterwards.

In the sections that follow in this chapter, I will talk about each of the four dimensions in more detail. But before that, I want to talk about the human dimension and the need to collaborate widely, to generate a range of solutions.

Collaborate Widely

We are all, innately, pattern-seekers. We jump to conclusions as soon as we are able, even if there is scant evidence to support our conclusions.[2] A prehistoric ancestor, who was running towards his prey, had to decide quickly whether the object that he saw in his path was likely to be a stick or a snake. Overall, those who decided it was a snake were more likely to stay within the gene pool than those who decided it was a stick. Natural selection has programmed our minds to avoid, at first glance, anything that we perceive to be threats. We opt for what seems 'safest'.

Having jumped to a conclusion, research also shows that once we have settled on a plausible conclusion, we seek out evidence that confirms its validity and ignore counter-evidence, no matter how compelling.[3] Then, having arrived at a conclusion, we will go to a lot of trouble to ensure that our subsequent actions are consistent with our initial conclusion, especially if that conclusion has been shared with others.

All of this makes it difficult for us, as individuals, to see what might be regarded as a mistake by an independent observer. By far the best way to avoid this is to get an outside view, or preferably a wide range of diverse outside views, as illustrated by the M-PESA case study in Chapter 3. Soliciting differing views will greatly enrich the solution options that you generate.

But keep in mind that the people you engage to help you find solutions are also susceptible to jumping to conclusions. Everyone brings baggage laden with preconceptions and prejudices. This can be particularly true for people who have helped you to create the vision and who may have already started to form views and ideas about what the solution might be.

Because you want everyone to have an open a mind when generating solutions, there is natural tendency to want to quash premature solution ideas. Sometimes, however, proposers of these ideas take rejection as a personal affront. The emotional part of their brain takes charge and the partly formed solution idea becomes something to be defended. A better approach is to welcome solution ideas as they arise. The contributor feels acknowledged and conflict is less likely to occur later on, when the slower non-emotional part of the brain is in charge. And, of course, it's also quite possible that these premature solutions are in fact good solution ideas or contain the seeds of a good solution. An Affinity Map workshop, as described in Appendix A, is a good way of getting existing ideas on to the table.

In the M-PESA example, even though it wasn't possible to get everyone together in one place at one time, the team made strenuous efforts to involve people and groups with different skills, experience and viewpoints.

RUN SOLUTION WORKSHOPS

Organise one or more solution workshops with a diverse mixture of people who have different perspectives and skills.

If your project is relatively small or straightforward, this may take just a couple of hours. But if it is a big beast of a project, like M-PESA, it may take many workshops over many days or even weeks. Devote effort that is proportionate to the size of the project.

Whatever the project size, it is worth getting someone independent to facilitate the workshops. This allows you to participate without having to worry about running the workshop at the same time.

I usually like to run at least two workshops for projects because things usually arise in the workshop that need to be investigated. A second workshop allows time to carry out those investigations and also provides time for each contributor's subconscious to work on the information from the first workshop, helping to generate those 'aha!' moments that occur when taking a bath, cooking or taking exercise.

In addition, disarm the fight against preconceived solution ideas by getting solution ideas out on the table, brainstorming style. Instead of a guerrilla war against pet solution ideas, you will have a rich source of input to the solution creation process.

In Appendix A, I describe some tools that you can use to stimulate participation and interaction in solution workshops.

Business stakeholders are a rich source of IT-enabled business solution ideas. Stakeholders in areas such as operations, marketing and finance will have perspectives from within their own business and industry sector. In addition, curious business managers will be observing and networking with their peers in other industry sectors. They will be aware of solutions that have worked elsewhere and these are a great source of ideas.

Be aware that IT suppliers often field only their senior team members for the solution generation process. If you are using an external supplier, you may well find these people will not even be working on your project. This has a number of drawbacks:

- Lack of continuity from solution generators through to implementers.

- A narrow view, biased towards certain solutions and technologies.

- You miss out on a rich source of creativity from their other people.

- Those involved tell you what they think you want to hear.

I recommend that you ask your supplier to field a diverse team containing individuals who:

- will be working on the project;

- will not be working on the project;

- come from different disciplines, such as business analysis, development and testing;

- are at different levels of seniority in the organisation.

LOOK OUTSIDE YOUR ORGANISATION

If you are budgeting a lot of money for a solution, it is worth actively seeking out ideas from other industries. Ask yourself: what industry or company does this or something comparable really well? Seek out contacts and talk to them.

In the late 1990s, I was running a programme in retail banking to aggregate back-offices of stand-alone retail banking branches into processing centres. I dragged my boss around the country to visit car and carpet factories that had reputations for world-class quality and customer service. Our visits played a major role in shaping our operating model for the new centres, particularly in terms of multi-skilling, team organisation, quality measurement and overall performance measurement.

Constraints

The solution generation process should begin with as few constraints as possible. In the M-PESA example, workshop attendees were told to 'assume that the technology can do anything you want it to'. This was good advice. Technology can usually do much more than most business people think it can. Without being aware of it, you could be imposing assumed constraints, based on limited experience or knowledge. Therefore, it is useful to take different perspectives when thinking about how the vision can be realised.

WHAT WOULD THE SOLUTION LOOK LIKE IF:

- You were on the bridge of Starship Enterprise?
- You were starting your business from scratch with limited funding?
- You were entering this business sector with limitless venture capital funding?

Because potential solutions are based on the vision, any constraints included in the vision will also apply to the solutions. However, it is not uncommon during the solution generation process for people to challenge these constraints, which have been 'inherited' from the vision. If that happens, you should revisit the vision. The constraints being challenged may have been imposed for a reason that you are not aware of or have forgotten. Don't just ignore them; find out why they are there and where necessary engage with stakeholders if you want to change or discard them.

There are three constraints that I recommend you consider at the start of solution generation:

1. Schedule.

2. Budget.

3. Regular value delivery.

The conventional way of thinking about IT projects is to choose a solution, then estimate how much it will cost and how long it will take: the linear approach. Sometimes, there is a desired delivery date, but the prevalent view of IT teams is that it will 'take as long as it takes' to deliver whatever is the agreed solution. If the business is firm about the date, IT management may insist that their teams come up with a plan that meets the 'required date'. When this happens, the IT team often lacks the commitment to achieve what they regard as an artificially aggressive date. The project either ends up 'late' relative to the desired date or the scope of what the project delivers is reduced at a later stage.

A better approach is to set a target schedule and budget at the beginning of the solution generation process. Rather than ask how much a particular solution will cost and how long it will take, set a budget and a schedule for achieving the vision. Challenge the solution generation team to come up with a range of solutions that fall within these constraints. That is exactly what happened with the Sony Walkman, which was discussed in Chapter 3. Setting a variety of budgets and delivery schedules can also be used as a thinking tool in order to generate solution options.

BUDGET AND SCHEDULE AS A THINKING TOOL

Ask for solutions that would achieve the vision:

- in three months;
- in six months;
- in a year;
- with a budget of X millions;
- with a budget of Y hundred thousands;
- with a budget of Z thousands.

The shorter and lower-cost scenarios might not deliver the full vision, but perhaps they deliver enough of it. Or perhaps they can stimulate creative thinking that can be used to create the chosen solution.

The reason that Chapter 4 (covering value-based delivery) preceded this one was because I wanted to make the case for regular value delivery before arriving here, so that I could recommend it be included as a constraint alongside the budget and time constraints. If you define the need for regular value delivery as a constraint at this point, then it can be built into the solution. It's a bit like IKEA insisting that any furniture design can be flat-packed.

Some other constraints may emerge during the solution generation process, as they did when defining a shared project vision. Let's say that Microsoft offered to donate software to the project for the homeless, mentioned earlier. One of the constraints might be that the solution has to use Microsoft software. Ordinarily, I would dismiss this as a technical specification consideration, but in this case it would be a high-level constraint on the business solution.

More often, implicit constraints based on false, untested assumptions creep into solutions unnoticed. They may manifest themselves as assumptions about what someone else thinks or the limits of what technology can do. However, introducing the idea of 'constraints' into the project's language helps make them explicit and visible, enabling you to challenge them and determine whether they are genuine.

KEEP A CONSTRAINTS LIST

Maintain a list of constraints, stating who suggested the constraint and why. This should not be a long list: perhaps 5–10 key constraints.

During workshops, have a large flip-chart-sized sheet of paper, headed 'Constraints', on the wall. This helps raise awareness that they are something that you need to capture. Often, it is easiest to capture them as they are articulated, rather than mine for them afterwards.

Define Performance Criteria Up-front

I once worked on a programme that opted for a solution that was based on a software package. In theory, the package had to be tailored to meet individual customer needs, but, in this instance, tailoring turned out to mean a lot of bespoke software development. After many months and many millions of pounds, the business people finally got their hands on the working software. Two problems were immediately evident: the new system was much slower than the existing system and it was more difficult to use. This is a common experience, especially in large organisations.

In this example, the problematic software would never have been purchased if appropriate performance criteria had been defined before the solution was chosen. In general terms, the criteria might have said that the new solution needs to be:

- as fast as the current solution;

- as easy to use as the current solution;

- more flexible than the current solution.

But performance criteria are not just about IT system performance; they also apply to business performance. For example:

- the maximum time taken to open an account;

- the maximum time taken to process an order;

- the acceptable number of incorrect transactions;

- the maximum cost of settling an insurance claim.

The key to defining useful performance criteria is quantification. Even something as apparently subjective as 'ease of use' can be quantified. It might, for example, be broken into component parts:

- number of training hours needed to attain a testable level of proficiency;

- numbers of errors per thousand transactions;

- average time in minutes to complete a transaction.

The author and thinker Tom Gilb[4] advocates an approach that brings rigour to the measurement of things that are usually left unmeasured. He suggests that we define a 'scale' and 'test' for the measure.

For example, the number of errors per thousand transactions is at first glance pretty unambiguous. It's certainly better than saying 'ease of use'. However, the 'number of errors per thousand transactions' could be measured (or 'tested') in a variety of ways, such as:

- a weekly sample of 100 transactions on a Wednesday morning;

- a daily sample of 300 transactions taken at random times;

- two daily samples of 25 transactions.

In Gilb's terms, we have:

- a scale of measurement: number of errors per thousand transactions;

- a test to determine where we are on that scale: a daily sample of 300 transactions taken at random times.

Gilb further suggests adding context by stating levels of performance:

- current level;

- worst level;

- best ever level;

- acceptable level;

- target level.

Continuing our ease of use example, this might give us the following.

Ease of use: Dimension #1	
Scale	Number of errors per thousand transactions
Test	A daily sample of 300 transactions taken a random times
Current performance level	14%
Worst performance level	23% (December 2011)
Best performance level	11% (June 2012)
Acceptable performance	9%
Target performance level	7%

SETTING PERFORMANCE LEVELS PROVIDES A BASIS FOR SOLUTION TRADE-OFFS

Having target and acceptable levels is extremely useful in solution generation. In effect, it represents a trade-off range that can be used to compare alternative solutions. The cost differential between achieving the target and acceptable performance levels can be quite significant.

For example, a Web-based, off-the-shelf (otherwise known as 'cloud') solution may be a lot cheaper to buy and maintain than a custom-built solution, but does not meet the target performance level. However, if the cloud solution meets or is better than the acceptable performance level, you can consider cost and performance together, to decide which solution offers the best value. It is also possible that the acceptable level might is revisited if other dimensions, such as ease of use, prove to be sufficiently compelling. The key point is that you have defined the acceptable level in advance, so deviating from it is a conscious and visible trade-off choice.

Always ensure that you define performance criteria *prior* to generating solutions options. Generating them on the fly, alongside the solutions, means that they are more likely to reflect the solution rather than shape it.

Being rigorous about performance criteria can take a lot of work, especially if existing performance data isn't readily available. How much rigour you employ depends on how important it is to the success of your solution.

Let's say, for example, you want to buy a relatively inexpensive software package in order to process management accounts. You have determined that speed and ease of use are important performance criteria. Rather than seeking to quantify performance, you could arrange for prospective users of the software to visit sites where the software is already in use. Through seeing the software being used and talking to the people using it, the prospective users may conclude that it meets the required performance criteria. This may be all the rigour you need.

In this example, however, you did at least consider what performance criteria were important before settling on a solution. And you did undertake some form of evaluation, commensurate with the level of risk, to ensure that the performance criteria were met.

On the other hand, let's say your vision is for customers to open their own bank accounts online, without training and without resorting to technical support, thereby eliminating back-office staff. In this case, you may well want to be rigorous about things like:

- the optimal duration for the process (that will to avoid customers reaching for the telephone instead);

- the volume and duration of support calls by customers;

- the acceptable number of customer errors that result in back-office work;

- the target customer satisfaction level.

As with constraints, don't go overboard with the number of performance criteria; try to focus on those key criteria that will make the difference between success and failure. And, don't forget that if the performance criteria are important, you need to request that the solution is designed to provide data that enable you to monitor them.

EXERCISE: HOW WOULD YOU QUANTIFY FLEXIBILITY?

Increased flexibility is often stated as a key driver for system replacement projects. What does it mean in practice?

– As an exercise, think about how you might quantify flexibility?

Identify Key Assumptions

As mentioned in Chapter 4, most business cases depend on relatively few key assumptions. A successful outcome depends on being within the permissible range of values for those assumptions. Examples might include:

- the number of customers who will buy a product;

- the reduction in the number of errors;

- the reduction in the time taken to process a transaction;

- the number of people who will choose a particular sales channel;

- the price that customers are willing to pay;

- the number of customers who will buy the product more than once.

I have often seen these sorts of assumptions buried in the corner of a spreadsheet and not revisited after initial estimates have been made. Ranges of values become frozen as a single value. Yet a tweak to the value of an assumption, one way or the other, can yield a very different result. You could choose to characterise these types of assumptions as performance criteria. That's not a bad idea because, if you follow Tom Gilb's advice, you will specify an acceptable range of values. The important thing, however, is that they are visible and not buried in a long list.

VISIBLE BUSINESS CASE ASSUMPTIONS ARE CRITICAL TO SUCCESS

The assumptions upon which the business case depends should be written large and ringed in lights – metaphorically, at least. They should be explicit and visible.

> If they are visible, creative ways can be found to test them as quickly and cheaply as possible. Lash together pilot solutions with bubble-gum and string before you spend a lot of money. Customers can be surprisingly willing to participate in pilots if they think they are helping to shape the solution.

In addition to these types of numeric assumptions, there may also be binary (yes or no) assumptions upon which the solution depends. I once saw a project whose solution required data from five different organisations. It was assumed that these organisations would be happy to sell their data if the price was right. The project was about two-thirds of the way towards completion before someone was dispatched to negotiate a price. It turned out that three of the organisations refused to sell the data at any price. They believed that the transparency resulting from sharing the data would leave them at a competitive disadvantage.

It sounds incredible that such a thing could happen, but assumptions are often made in order to avoid holding up progress. This is fine, but if they are not captured and described explicitly, they can and do get lost. People working on a project at an early stage can forget to document and check crucial assumptions, and people joining later may not realise that there are untested assumptions waiting like time-bombs. Much later, the bad news breaks, with people muttering sentences that begin with the word 'surely'.

As I write this, private security company G4S is being dragged across the coals for its failure to provide sufficient numbers of security staff for the London 2012 Olympics. I heard the Chief Executive of G4S, Nick Buckles, being interviewed on the radio this morning. 'Surely', asked the interviewer, 'you must have known it wasn't possible to recruit staff that quickly, so close to the games?' Embarrassed silence was followed by bluster. Then the interviewer asked: 'Do all of the staff recruited so far speak good English?' After much beating about the bush, Buckles was forced to admit that he didn't know. 'Surely', asked the interviewer, 'a test of language skills was included on the assessment?' Buckles initially volunteered that applicants had to have the right to work in the UK before admitting that he really didn't know if a language test was part of the application process.

'Surely' is a hindsight word. Don't give anyone the opportunity to use it about your project. Ensure that key assumptions are captured separately from solution descriptions. As with constraints, have a sheet for assumptions up on the wall during workshops.

EXAMPLE – VALIDATING KEY ASSUMPTIONS

In the mid-1990s, before the Internet was prevalent, opening a bank account comprised a long-winded process of filling in forms. A customer would collect a form from a branch and hand it in at the counter. The form was then given to back-office staff to open the account. Forms were often filled in incorrectly and this meant going back to customers for more details or to clarify something they wrote. This might happen more than once. The net result was that opening an account could take a couple of weeks, with costly ping-pong communication between the customer and the bank branch. This got even worse as the back-offices of branches were aggregated into large processing centres in remote locations.

I was directing a programme whose mission was to save money and improve customer service by 'redesigning' bank processes. A brainstorming team of branch staff tackled the account opening process.

They came up with a solution where the customer would walk into a branch and sit down with a member of staff at a screen, where they would key in the details together. Clarifications would be made along the way and the customer could check whether details, such as name and address, were keyed in correctly. A credit check would be made automatically during the process and if the result was good, bank cards and cheque books would be ordered automatically. If not, the customer was politely declined. The internal IT team estimated that it would cost about £2 million to develop this solution.

There were a lot of assumptions to validate for this solution, including the following:

- Customers are willing to take 20 minutes out of their day to open an account in a branch.
- The number of customers willing to sit down for 20 minutes.
- It can be done in 20 minutes.
- Branches have sufficient private space.
- Branch staff would be available at busy times.
- It cut down on error rates to a specified number that would result in the estimated cost savings.
- It would improve customer satisfaction.

We had a pretty creative IT team, who put together a prototype to help validate these assumptions. It was a stand-alone PC with no connectivity to other systems. The connectivity, including credit scoring, was emulated by printing off details and getting a member of the development team to key them into a different system in the back office.

We ran pilots in five different branches and learned a lot from customer and staff feedback. Based on the pilots, we gave the go-ahead for the IT project, whose solution design reflected the feedback. We decided, however, to continue running the pilots, in parallel to the IT project, so that we could continue to monitor our assumptions. We also expanded the pilot to a five more branches. We were three months into the IT development when it became apparent that private space and staffing at key times were both major obstacles in some branches.

Perhaps we had just gotten lucky with premises and staffing in the initial pilot branches? We had to set about the task of reviewing premises and staffing at over 2,000 branches to determine the additional expenditure required to bring reality back within the assumptions.

Fortunately, the cost saving, multiplied across that number of branches, was still significant enough to justify the additional expenditure and the IT project continued to completion, all the while continuing with pilots at different branches. However, if at any time we found that the numbers didn't stack up, we would have cancelled the project, as the customer services benefits were not sufficient on their own to justify the cost of the project.

Incidentally, don't forget that financial appraisals of project viability should be made on the basis of benefits versus *future costs*. Money already spent should be excluded. If you are not familiar with this idea, take a look at the section on 'sunk costs' in the glossary in Appendix B.

Identify Key Risks

An assumption always has an associated risk. That associated risk is that the assumption proves to be false. Assumptions can therefore always be expressed as risks. But I don't think that you should express every assumption as a risk as well as an assumption; this is just duplication. I favour expressing assumptions as such because the different terminology stimulates the mind to approach the subject from a different perspective. If, subsequently, you decide to reframe assumptions as risks, then that's fine.

Because risk is another perspective, it is worth thinking about risks as a separate item from assumptions. In my experience, assumptions come up naturally during the thinking process when generating solutions. Risks, however, seem to require effort to get people to think about them. But this effort is handsomely repaid. I believe that surfacing and dealing with risks throughout the project is one of the critical success factors for IT projects. You can identify risks by asking questions such as:

- What could go wrong?

- What's the worst that could happen?

- What could cause it to happen?

As with assumptions and constraints, I suggest that you try to capture risks during the solution generation process on a headed flipchart sheet on the wall of the workshop. However, I also like to run separate risk workshops for the favoured solutions.

To break down risks into their possible causes, I recommend the 'Fishbone diagram' (also known as an 'Ishikawa Diagram' after its inventor, Japanese university professor Kaoru Ishikawa).[5] It's a technique that originated in Japanese manufacturing and is designed a structured brainstorming tool to identify causes of problems. The drawing in Figure 5.2 below is an example of an online bank account opening solution.

Start by gathering suggestions for the answer to 'what's the worst thing that could happen?'. Tackle each one in turn by writing at the right-hand side of

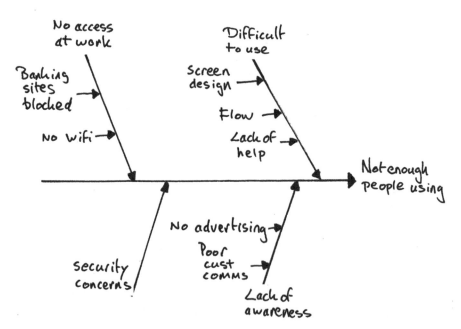

Figure 5.2   Fishbone diagram

the page. Then draw the central arrow, or backbone, from left to right, ending at the description of the problem. Now get people to suggest ideas for what caused the problem and draw them as arrows, arriving at the backbone. Each of these arrows can be further decomposed on sub-branches. Some people like to add category arrows to the backbone before brainstorming, as in Figure 5.2. You can, of course, choose your own categories.

The decision psychologist Gary Klein has suggested an alternative approach that he calls the 'pre-mortem'.[6]

WHAT IS A PRE-MORTEM?

A post-mortem is designed to establish the cause of death when a patient has died. A pre-mortem for a project is the 'hypothetical opposite'. It is carried out before 'the patient has died'. The idea is to step into the future and imagine that the project has gone very badly wrong. Perhaps it has turned into one of the black swans referred to in Chapter 2?

It seems that positioning ourselves in an imagined future and looking backwards to see what went wrong causes our minds to work differently from when we look forwards and ask what could go wrong. Looking backwards from an imagined future works well for the same reasons that a shared vision is so powerful. We are able to conjure up the movie of that future in our minds and with it all of the subconscious associations of project failures that we have experienced or heard about.

A pre-mortem is run as a workshop. Team members are gathered together and asked to put themselves into the future, by a timeframe appropriate to the project, and imagine that the project has been a disaster. They are given a few minutes to close their eyes and imagine it. What will people be hearing, seeing and feeling? Then, without conferring, each writes down the key causes of the failure. The meeting facilitator then asks each team member in turn to contribute a cause, capturing on a flip-chart or whiteboard, to be visible to all. Klein says:

> Although many project teams engage in pre-launch risk analysis, the pre-mortem's prospective hindsight approach offers benefits that other methods don't. Indeed, the pre-mortem doesn't just help teams to identify potential problems early on. It also reduces the kind of damn-the-torpedoes attitude often assumed by people who are over-invested in a project. Moreover, in describing weaknesses that no one else has mentioned, team members feel valued for their intelligence and experience, and others learn from them. The exercise also sensitises the team to pick up early signs of trouble once the project gets under way. In the end, a pre-mortem may be the best way to circumvent any need for a painful post-mortem.

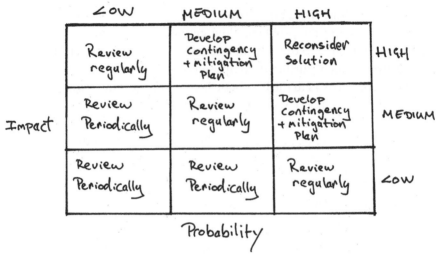

Figure 5.3   Risk matrix

When you have identified your risks, it is good discipline to assign each a probability of it happening and the impact if it does occur. I like to keep this simple by assigning a 'score' of high, medium or low to each dimension.

At the solution generation stage, you can draw a risk matrix such as the one in Figure 5.3 above and populate it with Post-it notes to get a feel for the risk profile of each of the solutions. It should be obvious that if the probability of the problem happening is high and the impact is high, you should seriously think about whether this is a viable solution.

Risks that are some combination of high and medium also require special attention. There are two key questions to ask:

- What can I do to reduce the probability and/or impact?

- Do I need a contingency plan (a plan B) in place in case the problem highlighted by the risk becomes reality?

You can decide to accept the other categories of risk, but as you move into delivery, you need to ask the same questions, especially with respect to probability. Something that is unlikely to happen today might be likely tomorrow because of a change in your company, your industry or the general business environment. Ensure that you review these risks regularly during delivery if you decide to live with them.

A couple of final thoughts on risk. First, I have seen people score impact and probability on scales of 1 to 5, or 1 to 10, or even percentages. If this is what your organisation does, then go with the flow. Personally, I don't see how that greater granularity of measurement helps, unless you take distinctly different action for the different scores. It's what you do about it that matters, not what you score. And you certainly don't want to waste time debating whether something is a 7 or an 8.

Second, some people recommend that risks are quantified in financial terms. Let me use security at the London 2012 Olympics again as an example. Nick Buckles of G4S said publicly that the company will lose about £50 million on the contract to supply security staff. Much of this comes from G4S having to foot the bill for the cost of army and police personnel who were needed to make up the shortfall of staff that were supposed to be supplied by G4S but were not. Good risk practice for G4S would have been to consider the probability of a shortfall and attach a cost to it.

I have no idea of the real numbers, but let's say that for every person short of the number it was contracted to provide, G4S loses £1,000 and has to pay £1,000 for an army replacement (both over the duration of the games). That's a cost of £2,000 for every individual below target. The risk assessment might look like this.

Table 5.1   Quantified risk assessment for security personnel shortfall

Shortfall	Probability of shortfall	Cost
100	90%	£2,000 x 100 x 0.9 = £180,000
+400 = >500	60%	£180,000 + (£2,000 x 400 x 0.6) = £660,000
+500 = >1,000	30%	£660,000 + (£2,000 x 500 x 0.3) = £960,000

A way of thinking about it is: what's the cost of plan B and what's the probability of having to invoke it?

In the case of G4S, the reputational damage to the company is likely to lead to even more substantial financial losses on other contracts. According to news reports, the shortfall in Olympic security personnel is at least 3,500. Appearing, live on television, before the government's Home Affairs Select Committee, Buckles said that G4S had taken on the contract to enhance the company's reputation rather than for financial gain. But he was then forced to concede that this very public failure was a 'humiliating shambles'. There are already calls to review the £230 million of existing police contacts and a further £300 million of other government contracts.

Whether you try to quantify risk in financial terms depends on the size of your project and the magnitude of the risk. I would suggest that it's a good discipline to attempt for your chosen solution, because it will, at least, stimulate another perspective on risk. I wonder if G4S ever asked 'what's the worst that can happen?'.

Use Terminology That Works for You

Capturing important information and making it visible is more important than categorising it. If you are organising solution workshops, which I recommend that you do, I have already suggested that you have flip-chart pages on the wall for each of following:

- constraints;

- performance criteria;

- assumptions;

- risks.

Don't waste energy and time debating which category something fits into. As long as you have stimulated thinking by taking each perspective, it doesn't really matter whether it is an assumption or a risk as long as you capture it and use it as a basis for action. Similarly, a constraint such as 'budget' could be described as a performance criterion, while a performance criterion such 'the time taken to process a transaction' could be described as a constraint or an assumption. That's fine. Capture it somewhere and do it once.

Before leaving this discussion, it would be remiss not to mention a fifth category that I could have used as one of the dimensions: that of 'business benefit'. In the section on performance criteria above, I used 'number of errors per thousand transactions' as an example. This could be described as a business benefit, expressed as 'a reduction in the number of errors per thousand transactions from 7 per cent to 14 per cent', for example. I prefer using the term 'performance criteria' rather than 'business benefit' or 'assumption'.

This is because performance criteria are things usually stated in advance that have to be met by a solution, whereas benefits tend to be thought of as flowing from a solution and therefore deduced afterwards. This is another example of stimulating the mind to work from a different perspective.

If, however, the common language in your organisation is to talk about benefits, I don't suggest that you engage in a major semantic battle. If people don't warm to the concept of performance criteria, then go with something like 'target benefits' – but if you do, ensure that they are introduced at the start of solution generation, not as a byproduct of it.

Compare the Value Offered by Different Solution Options

I have worked in some organisations where performance criteria are always turned into an explicit financial benefit, typically an increase in revenue or a cost saving. If this is the case for you, then value can be expressed simply as financial benefit divided by cost. More likely, as discussed in Chapter 3, projects deliver a bundle of performance criteria (or benefits) that, together with the cost, represent value.

An approach that can work well is to break a solution into its components and see how each contributes to the overall value.[7] Below is a hypothetical

Table 5.2   Solution component contributions towards key value dimensions

	Sexy	Internet	Ease of use	Speed of use	Cost ($)
Sliding keyboard	50%		90%	70%	a
Virtual keyboard	90%		70%	70%	b
Rollerball mouse	10%		50%	80%	c
Touch-screen	100%		100%	100%	d
Glass screen	90%				e
Plastic screen	60%				f
Optimised browser	30%	90%	20%	30%	g
Device specific applications	75%	75%	80%	80%	h
Weight <160 g	70%				i
Weight <140 g	90%				j
Thickness <12 mm	80%				k
Thickness <10 mm	90%				l

example for the Apple iPhone. The column headings are the performance criteria, which would have already been defined and quantified elsewhere, and the row names are the solution components. The percentages scores are arbitrary scores guessed at by the team that are meant to give a feel for the level of contribution that each solution component makes.

Having listed all of the solution options, you can then bundle them into alternative solutions, as illustrated in the table below below.

Table 5.3   Grouping of solution components into one solution option

	Sexy	Internet	Ease of use	Speed of use	Cost ($)
Virtual keyboard	90%		70%	70%	b
Touch-screen	100%		100%	100%	d
Glass screen	90%				e
Device specific applications	75%	75%	80%	80%	g
Optimised browser	30%	90%	20%	30%	h
Weight <130 g	90%				j
Thickness <12 mm	80%				k
Total coverage	*555%*	*165%*	*270%*	*280%*	*(b+d+e+g+h+j+k)*

The total coverage numbers are just a way of showing the contribution for a particular performance criterion. 'Sexy' obviously cannot contribute 555 per cent; it simply indicates that the particular dimension appears to be well covered. The process of thinking through the relative contributions is more important than the numerical result.

When evaluating the relative desirability of options, however, you also want to take into account the degree of risk associated with each option. If you have followed the advice given in this chapter, each solution option would also have a different profile of:

- cost;

- constraints;

- performance criteria;

- assumptions;

- risks.

The level of constraint, assumption and risk are all expressing risk in one way or another. You can use them to populate a matrix that compares the solutions side by side. In the table below, I have scored each dimension from one to five, where five is the most desirable score. Lower cost, for example, equals a higher score. You can either use this matrix in combination with the performance criteria matrix or on its own as separate thinking tool.

Table 5.4   Comparison of differing solution options

	Solution 1	Solution 2	Solution 3	Solution 4
Cost	4	3	3	1
Constraints	1	3	4	5
Performance criteria	2	4	4	4
Assumptions	1	3	2	4
Risks	5	4	3	2
Total	*13*	*17*	*16*	*16*

In this example, solution 2 has the highest score so would be the favoured option. This assumes, however, that the dimensions have equal weighting, which might not be the case. If cost were more important than the other dimensions, you might choose to double all of the cost scores. Conversely, you might decide to halve the constraints scores.

Don't get too hung up on the scores or exactly how you can get the two matrices to work together. The goal is to slow down thinking and view the solutions from different perspectives, not to have a universal scoring approach that does the thinking for you. The final choice will be one of management judgement.

Risks of Different Solution Types

I want to close this chapter with a few words of advice regarding the different IT solution types that might be proposed to achieve your business solution. There are essentially three options:

1.   Build something new.

2.   Extend the capability of something that already exists.

3.   Buy something ready-made, off the shelf.

NEW VERSUS REFURBISH

Building something completely new is proposed far too often. You hear your IT supplier say something like:

> The existing system is very old and difficult to maintain. We can replace it with the latest whizz-bang technology and you will have a much better system that is more flexible and cheaper to maintain.

Exercise great caution whenever you hear something like this. Who in their right mind demolishes their existing house and builds a new one just because they want a bigger kitchen? Refurbishment *is* possible for IT systems, just as it is for a home. What is often lacking is the will to consider refurbishment as an option. And if one really does need something completely new, just like a house, refurbishment can, over time, lead to something that is effectively new from top to bottom. However, it is done in stages, with existing value still in place, so it offers a much lower risk.

INSIST THAT THERE IS A REFURBISHMENT OPTION

There are cases when a completely new system is justified. But whenever this option is proposed, insist that a serious refurbishment option is proposed alongside this.

There are two ways of determining whether the refurbishment option has been seriously considered:

1. Get an outside view. This is the best approach, although it is not always politically acceptable. But if you are going to be spending a lot of money, you should seriously consider it.

2. Count the number of words or pages that the IT supplier has used to describe each option: new system versus refurbishment. It's not a very scientific test, but the volume of description is often a reflection of the amount of thought given to a topic.

Off-the-Shelf Solutions

These come in a variety of guises, from a fully-fledged business solution accessed via the Internet to a component of the business solution installed on your own premises. My advice for any solutions on this scale is the same.

> **TAILOR THE BUSINESS TO THE SOLUTION, NOT THE SOLUTION TO THE BUSINESS**
>
> I have seen an awful lot of money spent trying to tailor solutions to existing business processes. Off-the-shelf packages offer good value when you accept them as they are and tailor your business to fit them.

There is another class of solution that doesn't work straight out of the box. Such solutions are designed as a 'kit' that needs to be tailored to meet the customer's needs. Perhaps the best known of these is the Enterprise Resource Planning (ERP) system supplied by European software giant SAP. For these types of solution, it is important to find a way of figuring out the business and IT implementation costs. These can be considerable, so be sure to visit some people who have already installed it and are working with it in order to get the benefit of their experience and a handle on the total cost of ownership.

Overall, I am in favour of off-the-shelf solutions. Back in May 2003, Nicholas Carr wrote a controversial article in the *Harvard Business Review*, entitled 'IT Doesn't Matter'.[8] Essentially, he said that business processes are increasingly becoming commoditised. Therefore, unless your own software genuinely gives you a competitive advantage, buy it from a world-class supplier who will maintain and develop it on your behalf at a predictable cost. Since Carr wrote his article, the pace of commoditisation has quickened markedly, especially as 'cloud' solutions have matured (for an explanation of 'cloud', see the glossary in Appendix B).

Key Points from this Chapter

- Specify constraints and performance criteria at the start of solution generation.

- Set constraints for budget, schedule and taking a value-based delivery strategy.

- Quantify business and IT system performance criteria.

- Solution generation is an iterative process, with trade-offs between constraints, performance criteria, cost, assumptions and risks.

- Capture constraints, performance criteria, cost, assumptions and risks for each solution option.

- The language that we use stimulates different perspectives, but don't be dogmatic about what fits in which category.

- Select the preferred solution option based on value.

The figure below pulls together the ideas from this chapter and those given in Chapters 3 and 4.

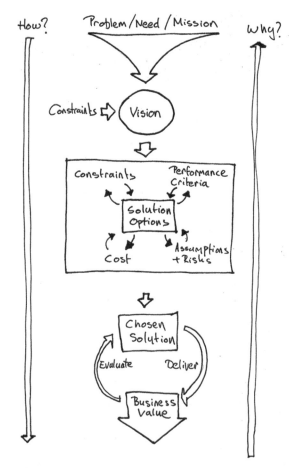

Figure 5.4   End-to-end process

WHAT IF YOUR PROJECT IS ALREADY WELL UNDER WAY?

The minimum that you can do is to examine the value profile for the solution that is being developed:

- What are the constraints? Are they explicit and accepted?
- Have business and IT performance criteria been defined?
- What are the key assumptions? What and how will they be validated?
- What are the risks? What are the mitigation and contingency plans?

Asking these questions will help you to validate and define the value offered by the selected solution and its probability of success.

Depending on the cost of your project and the stage that it has reached, you may also want to consider whether it might be worth pursuing an alternative. Asking the following questions is a good starting point for doing this:

What would the solution look like if:

1. you were on the bridge of the Starship Enterprise?;
2. you were starting your business from scratch with limited funding?;
3. you were entering this business sector with limitless venture capital funding?

What solution could achieve the vision:

1. in three months?;
2. in six months?;
3. in a year?;
4. with a budget of X millions?;
5. with a budget of Y hundred thousands?;
6. with a budget of Z thousands?

You can also try using the one-minute health-check given in the Introduction.

6

The Business Case as a Management Tool

Rethinking the Role of the Business Case

Writing a business case is often viewed as a necessary evil, produced solely to get authorisation or funding for a project to proceed. Unless it is driven by some form of regulatory requirement, the financial case usually determines whether a project should be given the green light. Once the project is given the go-ahead, the business case is often filed away in a drawer and forgotten. This is a missed opportunity. Whatever the size of your organisation, a succinct, one- or two-page business case summary (such as the example in Figure 6.1 on the following page) can:

1. act as a reference point that describes the essence of the project from a business perspective;

2. be reviewed regularly, preferably monthly, to evaluate whether project is still viable and if it should continue;

3. keep attention on those things, such as the key assumptions and risks, that will determine the project's ability to deliver the vision.

For larger projects, when a business case is initially submitted for approval, this summary may need to be supplemented with additional material. That might include things such as a marketing plan, customer research, a business model, business process redesigns, detailed financial projections and a summary of the other options considered. The essence of the business case can, however, be summarised on one or two pages and this is what needs to be reviewed regularly. For smaller and medium-sized projects, the one or two pages may well suffice.

Project Vision for Online Personal Account Opening Project:					

Personal customers can open their own bank accounts online, from a PC or mobile device, without training and without resorting to technical support, thereby improving customer service and saving cost by eliminating back office staff.

Financial benefits (£000's NPV) calculated using discount rate of 9%

Target Case NPV: 541			Worst Case NPV: -107		

Target Case Cash-flow (£000's)

Year	0	1	2	3	4
Project Cost	-1500				
Operating Cost		-70	-70	-70	-70
Revenue		0	0	0	0
Cost Saving		700	700	700	700
Total	*-1500*	*630*	*630*	*630*	*630*

Performance criteria:
1. Customers can complete account application in no more than 15 minute.
2. Less than 20% of applicants telephone for support.
3. Less than 15% applicants make and error that results in back-off rework.

Key assumptions:
1. 30% of all applications will be self-completed by end of first year.
2. 50% of all applications will be self-completed by end of third year.
3. Web (HTML5) will be suitable for mobile devices

Key risks:
1. Security concerns put people off.
2. Difficult to use without help.
3. Applicants unaware they can apply online.

Key constraints:
1. Solution must cost no more that £2.5 million.
2. Annual running must be less that £300,000.
3. Solution must run on all types of PCs and mobile devices.

Outside Scope:
1. Business Accounts are not included.
2. Native mobile App is not included.
3. In-branch solution not included

Roles and responsibilities

Sponsor: Gary Lloyd	**Project Manager:** Doug Smith

Key stakeholders:
David Duckham (Head of Personal Banking) , Barry John (Head of online services), Sandy Carmichael (Chief Information Office), Bill McBride (Head of Customer Services)

Figure 6.1   Business case summary

This chapter will describe each of the sections within the business case summary. But before that, I want to say a little about the cultural challenge of establishing a regular business case review. A regular review acknowledges that:

- the business environment that gave rise to the business case may change;

- the business case is based on assumptions that may turn out to be invalid;

- the project may get blown sufficiently off-course such that it will no longer deliver the business case.

Most people will agree that if a project is no longer going to deliver its business case, it should be cancelled or, at least, undergo radical surgery; however, accepting that business cases are often inherently uncertain and in need of validation takes personal and organisational maturity. This is not to imply that organisations should recklessly take risks, but rather, that they should recognise and manage those risks, such that prompt action can be taken when necessary. Alas, in my experience, most organisations assume that the business case will be achieved unless something exceptional happens. Establishing a regular business case review therefore requires strong leadership.

Business Case Components

VISION

As discussed earlier in this book, a shared project vision is the foundation of a successful project. Keeping the vision visible, at the very start of the business case summary, reminds everyone of the project's 'true north'. In the regular business case review, it poses the following questions:

- Is what we have done so far consistent with the vision?

- Is what we have planned consistent with the vision?

- Are we still on course to achieve the vision?

- If the answers to any of these questions is 'no', then what should be done?

FINANCIAL CASE

Why the Financial Case is Important

There are two types of organisation when it comes to the financial case for a project. The first type insists on a robust financial case that is scrutinised in detail by the finance department. Projects without a good financial case have a tough time getting approved, unless it is absolutely clear that there is some other legal or regulatory need.

The second type of organisation doesn't bother too much with financial cases. Projects get sanctioned because someone in a position of power wants them done. There is sometimes a financial case, but it is usually superficial and cobbled together to satisfy the organisation's internal process. There is, of course, a spectrum between these two extremes, but approaches do seem to be polarised.

Even if you are in the latter type of organisation, I would still encourage you to define a robust financial case for your project. First, you want to be sure that your project is adding value and, second, if you believe in your project, you want to be able to defend it in prioritisation debates or in the event of a change in management ethos.

I recall a project, in an organisation in which I worked, that was sponsored by a powerful Chief Information Officer (CIO). He had little time for those who complained about the lack of a business case for his pet project. The project had been going a year when he resigned to take up a more prestigious role in another company.

Within a week of taking over, the replacement CIO called the management team together and asked 'where is the business case for *this thing*?'. A week later, the project was cancelled. There were 40 people working on the project, including two IT suppliers. Half of the staff on the permanent team were made redundant during the weeks that followed.

Format of the Financial Case

The best way of describing a financial case is as a Net Present Value (NPV). For those not familiar with the concept of an NPV, I have included a primer in Appendix C. In essence, an NPV aggregates future cash flows, of costs and benefits, and expresses them in today's money as a single number. This number shows how much financial value is added or subtracted by the project. The financial case should reflect the total cost of ownership, including post-project costs such as operating and license costs, rather than just the project development cost.

It's usual to show three scenarios: best, worst and target case. Often, however, this is a perfunctory exercise, similar to coming up with a mandated set of three options for the solution. It's a shame when this is the case because scenarios present an opportunity to link the financial scenarios to project uncertainty, as expressed in the project's assumptions and risks.

The scenarios should use combinations of more than one variable, not just a shortfall in revenue or cost savings. So, for example, a scenario might combine cost overrun, schedule overrun, underachievement of cost savings and the need to spend money on risk mitigation or contingency. This is best done not by merely tweaking numbers up or down, but by sitting down with the team to think about 'what will we do if this or that happens … what is the impact and how will we respond … and then what could happen?' – realistic, thought-through scenarios.

I like to include the worst-case scenario on the business case summary as this is the minimum that the project needs to achieve to be viable. I don't usually include the best-case scenario because it doesn't really add any value to decisions that might have to be made about the course of the project.

The Project Cost Conundrum

Stressing the importance of the financial case might seem to be at odds with my assertion in earlier chapters that estimates of the total project cost are more often wrong than right. So how does one deal with this conundrum? The best approach, as I alluded to at the start of this chapter, is to accept that the cost estimate is uncertain and will change as the project progresses. In place of false certainty about the cost, take a realistic risk management approach.

At the outset of the project, set a budget constraint for project cost and use this value in the initial NPV calculation. Then, if you follow a strategy of regular value delivery, you will start to get a handle on the IT supplier's productivity by comparing estimated and actual costs for each successive delivery of value. This enables you and your supplier to refine the overall cost estimate and revise the NPV calculation. In this way, the financial case is alive and subject to scrutiny throughout the life of the project rather than being unrealistically set in stone.

Performance Criteria

The performance criteria were described in the previous chapter. In business case summary format, suggested above, I have limited the number of performance criteria to three. Those listed are meant to represent the key criteria that drive the business case and might include things like the following:

- Achieve x number of customers purchasing through mobile apps.

- Achieve x per cent repeat purchases from customers who have bought once in stores.

- Errors per thousand business accounts opened to be no more than y per cent.

- y per cent of customers say they would recommend product z to friends.

If your list seems too long, try arranging them into a hierarchy that allows them to be summarised. For example:

- The number of children under the age of five who die because of contaminated drinking water to be less than z per cent of the population for the target area.

    - the proportion of drinking needs satisfied by rainwater harvesting:

        - rainfall harvested in centimetres;
        - weekly water consumption in litres;
        - water lost through evaporation in centimetres.

    - the number of families using the container effectively:

        - the number of storage containers delivered;
        - the number of families within two hours' walk of the distribution point;

○   the proportion of families who collect a container from distribution point;

○   the number of families still using the container after six months.

As I mentioned in the previous chapter, you can, if you prefer, describe the performance criteria in terms of benefits, sometimes described as non-financial benefits. To some, this will seem to be more natural terminology for a business case. I have no issue with flipping terminology as long as 'non-financial benefits' are quantified in the same rigorous way as performance criteria. Unless you can measure whether something is achieved, it is unlikely to get done. If you are not sure how to do this, go back and take a look at the section on performance criteria in Chapter 5.

Even though you have expressed the performance criteria, or non-financial benefits, as an item that is distinct from the financial benefits, you should still make every effort to express the impact of achieving the performance criteria in financial terms and include it in your NPV. For example, if a particular performance criterion will reduce the number of errors, try to estimate the cost per error and thus the financial saving. If the performance criterion is about disease prevention, try to find out whether there are costs, such as the cost of treatment, that would be avoided through early screening.

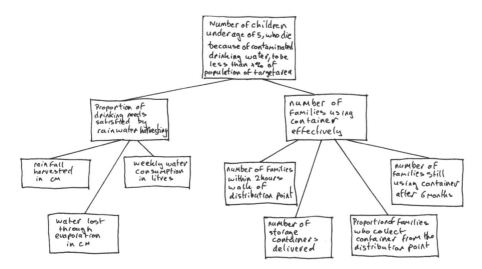

Figure 6.2   Hierarchy of performance criteria

KEY ASSUMPTIONS

In previous chapters I talked about the need to identify assumptions upon which the business case depends; keeping them visible in the business case summary helps to ensure that they are regularly revisited. This point is so important that I want to reinforce it with another example.

Let's assume that you are responsible for a project for an insurance company whose goal is to reduce the number of errors made when keying in paper-based claims. To turn this into a financial benefit, you need to know how many fewer errors are likely to be made as a consequence of the project. You also need to know the cost of making an error. Each of these represents an assumption. At the very start of the project, these types of assumptions may be no more than educated guesses, indicating whether the idea is worth pursuing. As we progress through the project, you should be seeking to validate these assumptions.

Initially, you might undertake some sampling to find out the current error rate. You might then follow the life of a sample of transactions, identifying the cost components of making an error, such as dealing with the customer and correcting the information supplied. You could go even further and investigate the impact of errors on customer satisfaction and the consequent impact on customer retention and thus revenue. These would be further assumptions that you could seek to validate. For now, let's keep it simple and restrict ourselves to two assumptions: errors and their direct cost.

Note that at this point in the project, we have yet to contemplate any solutions. Our next step could be to define a performance criterion that we want to achieve. Say we want to reduce the number of errors from X to Y, thereby saving our organisation £Z. Let's say that the project team considers a range of options and settles on a solution to use optical character recognition in order to capture the information from the forms. The cost of the new solution is estimated and provides a positive NPV over a five-year timeframe. The business case is proposed and accepted.

At this point, the following key assumptions are in play:

1.   The reduction in the volume of errors.

2.   The cost per error.

3.   The volume of paper-based claims.

However, let's say that because of customer complaints, non-IT initiatives are being pursued to reduce the extent of the problem. These include a redesign of the paper form and customers being offered a discount on future premiums if claims are made online. In addition, prompted by the project's analysis of the cost of errors, a local initiative changes the back-office business process to make it more efficient.

Although these initiatives might be taken into account in the business case, if they are more successful than anticipated, the viability of the business case might be affected. If we monitor the key assumptions regularly, over time, we can evaluate whether the project still delivers value. If we do not monitor the assumptions regularly, the project is likely to carry on regardless.

You might think that it would be obvious to review the impact of the complementary non-IT changes. In large organisations, however, local frontline initiatives can easily become detached from big head office IT initiatives. Sometimes, head office will keep an eye on the impact of the local initiatives for the first month, but will lose interest unless the immediate impact is high. The snowball effect that occurs as frontline changes are refined can easily be overlooked.

KEY RISKS

As with the list of assumptions, this section should list the key risks that could make or break the project. If you followed the advice in the previous chapter, you should simply be able to list the top risks here so that they are visible and regularly monitored.

As stated in the previous chapter, assumptions can always be expressed as risks. But simply rewording the assumptions already listed in the business case summary as risks is a waste of time. Make completion of the business case a thinking exercise, not a form-filling exercise. If you have thought hard about risks, you should be able to list some top risks that are distinct from the assumptions.

KEY CONSTRAINTS

Like the previous sections on assumptions and risks, constraints should be things that are critical for the project. These are the constraints that the project has to observe in order to remain viable. They are the ones that, if broken, should prompt a serious review of the business case and whether the project should continue.

Two of the key constraints that are listed should be the budget available and when the solution is needed, along with any intermediate value delivery dates.

OUTSIDE SCOPE

One of the biggest complaints that I hear about IT projects is that the project didn't deliver what people thought it would. A friend of mine who acts as an expert witness in legal disputes about IT projects tells me that project scope is one of the most frequent causes of disputes.

The most effective way of clarifying what is within scope is to list those business outcomes that are *not* within the scope. This is because people will often assume that their own desires will be met by the project's vision. You could, as some projects do, make a long list of what is within and outside scope. However, busy people are unlikely to read these types of lists and are more likely to jump to conclusions in terms of what is *in* scope, without much investigation.[1]

Listing what is outside scope in terms of *business outcomes*, rather than long lists of features, engages people at the level of the vision and is succinct enough to be visible in the business case summary. Let's say, for example, that your project's vision is to allow people to make small value payments to shopkeepers using mobile phones. You might state 'payments between individuals is outside scope'. It's a simple short statement that engages thinking at the vision level.

ROLES AND RESPONSIBILITIES

Project Sponsor

I recommend naming the sponsor in the business case summary so that everyone knows who it is. Sometimes the role will change hands during a project, so naming the sponsor also ensures that everyone knows who is currently fulfilling the role, rather than who was in the role at the beginning of the project.

Project Manager

The identity of the project manager is not always obvious to the stakeholders. And, just like the sponsor, the person fulfilling the role may change, so it is good to keep the name visible.

I recall being asked to review a project by one of its senior stakeholders. About halfway through my first Steering Group meeting, I passed a note to my client. My note prompted him to ask 'so who is in overall charge of this project?'. A couple of names were volunteered, but it turned out that they were only responsible for certain aspects of the project. The truth was that there was no-one in overall charge of the project.

It is always worth making clear who is in charge in the one-page business case summary.

Key Stakeholders

Managing stakeholders throughout the life of a project is absolutely vital for success. Even well-run projects that have identified and engaged with key stakeholders at the beginning can lose sight of who they are and their needs as the project progresses. Having them named on the business case summary ensures that they are always in mind. Of course, you cannot name every single stakeholder, but you should, at least, list those we described in Chapter 3 as having a high degree of both power and interest.

My preference is to name individuals, together with their roles, wherever possible. Effective stakeholder management depends on building relationships between people, not between roles. Always specifying named individuals is a reminder of this. In addition, it helps to identify when changes of responsibility occur and communicates those changes with the other stakeholders.

Business Case Red Flags

By the time you complete your business case summary, there is a risk that you will be in love with your project, or at least very fond of it. It will have a good NPV, it will deliver great performance and although one or two key risks are highlighted, you were smart enough to spot them and devise credible mitigation and contingency plans. Not only that, but you have crafted your business case summary to sit perfectly on a single page – it looks good.

Now is the time to slow down your thinking and look at your business case objectively. Unfortunately, as Daniel Kaheman tells us,[2] it is difficult for us to spot our own mistakes. A solution is therefore to enlist independent reviewers who have three qualities:

1.   They must be independent of you and the project.

2.   Your must respect their judgement.

3.   They must be honest.

The last of these is the toughest to achieve. In the main, if you respect someone's judgement, you will like them and this will be reciprocated. The corollary is that people who like you will not want to hurt your feelings and will, as a consequence, soften their blows, despite any entreaty to be brutally honest. They know that what you really want to hear is that the business case is great, with perhaps one or two relatively minor things that need to be addressed.

Assuming you choose a reviewer, or better still more than one reviewer, that you like, you can help them remain objective by providing a simple checklist of business case weaknesses to look out for. As an aside, in his book *The Checklist Manifesto*,[3] Atul Gawande calls on his experience as a surgeon and as an advisor to the World Health Organization to describe the literally life-saving power of simple checklists – not long bureaucratic checklists in the hands of dummies, but succinct checklists in the hands of experts. 'They provide a kind of cognitive net', writes Gawade. 'They catch mental flaws inherent in all of us – flaws of memory and attention and thoroughness'.

My suggestion to you is that you write your own checklist before you write the business case. This will have the effect of pre-arming you against those mental flaws of memory, attention and thoroughness. To help you on your way, below are some common red flags that I look for in business cases.

BUSINESS CASE CHECKLIST

- Is the vision clear?
- Is the scope unambiguous?
- Have the key stakeholders been identified and engaged?
- How was the cost saving or increased revenue calculated and tested?
- Is the worst-case scenario really the worst case in terms of project cost, operating costs and cost savings/revenue?

- Does the project cost include contingency for change and for maturing risks?
- What is the change budget?
- What is the risk budget?
- Does the project cost include all of the non-IT costs, such as training, premises and staffing?
- Does the NPV include all operating costs, such as licensing, infrastructure and staffing?
- Is the discount (or hurdle) rate visible and does it reflect the risk of the project?
- What are the comparators that were used to calculate the discount rate?
- Is the time horizon used to calculate the NPV realistic?
- Are the performance criteria realistic?
- Are they wishful thinking or based on something concrete?
- What key risks are missing?
- What key assumptions are missing?

Key Points from this Chapter

- The essence of a business case can be summarised in one or two pages.

- Describe what is out of scope in terms of business outcomes.

- The business case should be reviewed regularly, preferably monthly.

- Business cases are often inherently uncertain and need validation.

- A regular business case review acknowledges that circumstances and assumptions may change.

- Regularly reviewing whether a project should continue will be a cultural shift for many organisations.

WHAT IF YOUR PROJECT IS ALREADY WELL UNDER WAY?

Whatever stage you are at, you can always create a business case summary and add it to the monthly review process. If you don't have a monthly review, the business case summary can be created and used to drive that review.

Most likely, you will find that the exercise of constructing the business case summary will highlight areas that have not been well defined or, perhaps, have not been considered at all. Thus, writing the business case summary will effectively be a review of what the project is seeking to achieve and whether it is on course, something that is worth doing at any stage of a project.

7

Project Delivery

At the outset of this book, I stressed that proactive business leadership *throughout* a project is the key to success. The job isn't done when the ship sets sail, just because it is pointing the right direction. However, the majority of this book may seem to be devoted to pointing the ship in the right direction rather than sailing it. But my goal has been to do more than that. The tools suggested in this book serve a dual purpose – they define the direction, but they also provide you with a set of instruments to help you stay on course and get you safely to your desired destination. You need to have a compass on board when you set sail.

As I have said before, the task of business leadership for an IT project is not to micro-manage the IT supplier. In this chapter, I will recommend a number of touchpoints, where you should sit down with your supplier to review the progress and health of the project. I recommend two types of touchpoints that I will explain in detail in the following sections. They are:

- When value is delivered – the touchpoints when you have the opportunity to evaluate and adjust.

- Regular reviews meetings – the touchpoints that determine whether you are on course, whether anything is likely to blow you off course and what should be done about it.

Value Delivery

Value delivery is an opportunity for evaluation across four key dimensions:

1. Business case assumptions.

2. Actual performance versus the schedule and cost estimates.

3.   Quality and performance criteria for specific value delivery.

4.   Customer-supplier relationship.

I have touched on all of these in one way or another in previous chapters. Most are self-evident but I want to emphasise the first of these because it is so important during delivery; all too often, when a project's underlying business case assumptions turn out to be incorrect, the news is met with a shrug of the shoulders, an expression of disappointment, but no action. However, unless the assumptions were flimsy in the first place, this is the time for persistence. You want to understand why the assumptions have turned out to be invalid and what can be done about it.

Take the example of opening bank accounts online that I described in Chapter 5. A key business case assumption is the number of people who are willing to open accounts online. When an account is opened online, a customer is effectively doing the work instead of a member of staff. The resulting accumulation of cost savings from opening many accounts pays for the project, plus a surplus saving.

The first step in realising value is to monitor the business case assumption from the moment of delivery and to monitor whether the trend is heading in the right direction. In this example, therefore, you should monitor the adoption trend from the outset and extrapolate to see whether the target is likely to be reached. If target is likely to be missed, you should make every effort to find out why. You might ask questions such as the following:

- Was the underlying research flawed and, if so, why?

- Are customers aware of the service?

- Is the solution too difficult to use?

- Are customers worried about security?

- What would encourage customers?

You have spent a lot of time and money to come this far; it's not the time to give up. Perhaps you need to spend some money to perform market research and find out why customers are not adopting it? Perhaps you need to spend money on promotion? This is a good example of the principle of sunk costs. The money spent on the project has gone and you cannot get it back. The question to ask now is how much do you have to spend to get the benefit, irrespective of what has already been spent? The job is not done once the capability is delivered. Getting value takes work, not faith.

REALISING VALUE

IT projects are expensive. To realise their value, you have to follow through. Are performance criteria being achieved and are key business assumptions proving to be correct? If not, why not? What could be done?

Sometimes you need to invest more to extract the value, regardless of how much has already been spent.

Regular Review Meetings

Even if you have established a pattern of regular value delivery, it's still important to review the overall health and direction of the project on a regular basis. I recommend a regular meeting, chaired by the project sponsor, to review the following points:

- Project progress and trajectory versus the business case summary.

- Key risks that were not included in the business case summary.

- Expenditure versus budget and progress versus schedule.

- Key issues arising that are not covered already by the above points.

The central purpose of the meeting is to take decisions and assign responsibility for actions that address matters arising from the agenda. Assigning responsibility and a timeframe for action is absolutely critical. I have frequently seen senior people make decisions in meetings only to be surprised that nothing happens as a consequence. Follow through is essential to make decisions stick.

WHAT IS A DECISION?

Management guru Peter Drucker, writing in the *Harvard Business Review* about 'What Makes an Effective Executive', wrote that:

> *A decision has not been made until people know:*
> - *The name of the person accountable for carrying it out;*
> - *The deadline;*
> - *The names of the people who will be affected by the decision and therefore have to know about, understand, and approve it – or at least not be strongly opposed to it – and*
> - *The names of the people who have to be informed of the decision, even if they are not directly affected by it.*[1]

The frequency of these 'steering' meetings should be determined by the value, risk and urgency of the project. If these are sufficiently high, you should want to meet very regularly, say weekly. I have seen this happen in small organisations and start-ups where the business owners want to be closely involved in the project – remember Steve Jobs and the iPhone? I have also seen a high level of frequency in large organisations in the early stages of design-thinking and process re-engineering projects.

In my experience, however, projects usually fall into two main categories, with some grey territory in between. There are large projects of six months or more that establish monthly steering meetings and there are projects of 12 weeks or less that establish a fortnightly or, sometimes, weekly steering meeting. But don't just slip into these familiar routines. Think about the mix of value, risk and urgency. How important is the project to you and how often do you want your hands on the steering wheel? There is nothing that says that the lunar cycle should determine the frequency of project steering meetings.

I recommend that steering meetings are chaired by the project sponsor and are attended by the key members of the project team, including the suppliers. If the sponsor is sufficiently senior, his or her presence will send a clear message that the project is important. Suppliers will want to field members of their team who are at a comparable level of seniority to the sponsor. This helps to ensure that actions arising from the review get addressed quickly.

Sponsors should chair, rather than simply attend, because this puts them in the driving seat, asking questions and seeking information. This is a role that most senior people are good at and relish, so it is a waste not to use that skill and experience. It puts other participants on their mettle and the dynamic of the meeting becomes one in which the sponsor is seen as the leader who is determined to ensure that the project delivers value, rather than just attending as an interested observer.

If a project has a sponsor who is unable or unwilling to get along to the formal meetings, the project sponsor is probably at the wrong level in the organisation or is sending a clear message that the project is unimportant. As I noted in Chapter 2, 'Stepping Up to the Plate', if organisations want to get value from their projects, they should appoint sponsors who have the time to take an active role and who are given the decision-making authority to fulfil their role.

Before discussing each of the agenda items for the steering meeting, I want to say a little about project team meetings. The steering meetings are important, but regular project team meetings that review, progress, issues and risks are the heartbeat of any project and provide the groundwork and information needed for successful steering meetings. If the steering meetings are monthly, I suggest you ensure that team meetings are taking place weekly.

I once inherited a project in trouble and was surprised to hear from the project manager that team meetings no longer took place 'because no one seemed to be interested'. It was little wonder that the project was in trouble and equally little wonder that the project manager eventually decided that project management wasn't his calling.

Ever since then, I always check that project team meetings are taking place and that they are effective. My effectiveness test is simple:

- Is there a list of issues and risks, with owners?

- Is there evidence that risks and issues are being closed and new ones opened?

- Are there actions against issues and risks, with owners and due dates?

If project team meetings are the project management heartbeat, then risks and issues are the blood-flow and I want to see evidence that it is active and alive.

Business Case Summary

This area was thoroughly covered in Chapter 6, so rather than repeat it, I will make just one point, which is also general to the overall need for a formal monthly review.

An IT project can spend a lot of money in just a month. Stop and think for a moment about the number of people working on the project and the daily rate at which they are charged. A month represents 20 days for one person. Five people represent 100 days. If you are in financial services, the daily rate, including overheads, might be around £1,000 – that's a monthly cost of £100,000 for just five people! And many projects are much larger. Even if you daily cost is lower – say half – similar arithmetic will illustrate the magnitude of the risk being taken by skipping a monthly review. Think about how many products would need to be sold, or errors avoided, to pay for a month's worth of work on the project.

Therefore, it is vital that the monthly business case review does not turn into a perfunctory, box-ticking exercise.

Risks

The critical risks should have been reviewed as part of the business case summary. However, if you have conducted a thorough risk analysis, there will be other key risks that need to be reviewed regularly, along with new risks that emerge as the project progresses. The purpose of the monthly risk review is to identify and track actions that will reduce the probability and impact of key risks, and to devise and invoke a contingency plan where necessary. Typical questions to ask at the review are as follows:

- Has the probability or impact of the risk changed? If yes, why and what are the implications?

- Is the impact sufficiently high to warrant a contingency plan? If yes, has one been developed and what is the trigger for invoking it?

- Have actions been identified and assigned to reduce the impact and probability? If yes, what is their status?

- If not, what can be done, who should do it and by when?

The risk categorisation matrix that I introduced in Chapter 5 should help determine which risks need to be reviewed as part of the monthly review.

All risks that are 'life-threatening' to the project should be reviewed at least monthly. These include those risks that are categorised as 'develop

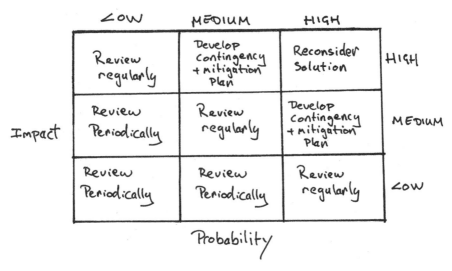

Figure 7.1   Risk matrix

contingency and mitigation plan' and 'reconsider solution'. Ideally, all other risks categorised as 'review regularly' should be reviewed monthly, but if the list is very long, they may need to be separated into those that will benefit from being addressed in the meeting and those that can be addressed outside of the meeting. If you are in doubt, include them in the meeting.

If the list is too long to get through in the meeting, this is either telling you that you have a very risky project or that the risks described are at too low a level of granularity. However, I would rather have a risk visible, to be able to make that judgement, rather than miss it by not including it. I like to use an open risk process, where there is a mechanism in place for anyone working on or affected by the project to be able to table a risk. It's a healthy project culture in which bad news travels fast. There should be no excuse for someone to say 'yes I knew it was a problem but no-one wanted to listen'.

Progress versus Schedule and Expenditure versus Budget

EARNED VALUE ANALYSIS IN A NUTSHELL

The graph shown in Figure 7.2, on the following page, is an example of a technique that allows progress against schedule and expenditure versus budget to be shown in a single image. The vertical axis is money. The horizontal axis is

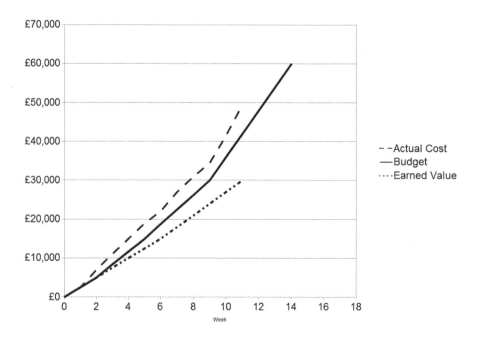

Figure 7.2   Earned value analysis with budget, actual and earned value

the project duration subdivided into time periods, usually in weeks or months, as appropriate for the project duration and cost.

The middle line, plotted on the graph, represents budget. The line above it represents actual cost and the line below it represents something known as 'earned value'. The overall approach is known as 'earned value analysis'. It is something that you can ask your supplier to provide for you.

The graph tells you that if the actual cost line is above the budget line, then the project is overspending. If the earned value line is below the budget line, it is behind schedule. In this example, the project is clearly over budget and behind schedule. Plotting these lines on a graph allows you to spot trends that are not immediately obvious with traditional milestone reporting and financial spreadsheets. It clearly shows that both actual cost and earned value are trending away from the budget line, indicating that things are likely to get worse not better. Indeed, it is a pretty simple exercise to extrapolate those lines in order to determine how much worse things might get.

While the relationship between actual cost and budget is pretty obvious, the idea of earned value is less intuitive. Therefore, although you will be asking your supplier to provide the graphs, it's a good idea for you to understand how it works so that you can understand better what you are looking at. The following section will take you through a simple worked example to show you how it works and some of the nuances that it is worth being aware of.

Before getting into the example, it is worth saying that earned value analysis is not dependent on having taken the regular value delivery approach that I advocate. It can be applied equally well to a waterfall-style project that is currently in progress and I will explain how as I go through the example.

CONSTRUCTING AN EARNED VALUE ANALYSIS – AN EXAMPLE

To make the example easy to follow, I am going to use a *Grand Designs*-style renovation project and restrict it to the initial stages rather than the whole project. In the example, I have assumed that the project is structured to deliver regular value, but this is not essential for the earned value approach to work. To keep things straightforward, I have assumed that items listed are completed sequentially, such that work doesn't start on the bathroom until the toilet is finished and so on. Here is the budget for the first four deliveries.

Table 7.1   **Budget for first four deliveries for *Grand Designs* example**

Description of value delivered	Week	Budget	Cumulative budget
Toilet	2	£5,000	£5,000
Bathroom	5	£10,000	£15,000
Bedroom 1	9	£15,000	£30,000
Kitchen	14	£30,000	£60,000

As each of the items, such as the toilet and the bathroom, is completed, we can say that value has been delivered. Now, if each of the items had an objective measure of financial value delivered, we could plot it on a graph that shows when it was delivered versus when we expected it to be delivered.

But how do we express the financial value of having the toilet or the bathroom? The earned value analysis solution is to express the value in terms of budgeted cost. So, when the toilet is delivered, we say that £5,000 of value has been 'earned'. When the bathroom is delivered, we say that £10,000 of value has been 'earned'. If you have grasped that intuitively, then you have done so much faster than I did the first time I came across the concept. If you found it tricky, I suggest you read it again and closely follow the step-by-step example over the following pages.

Let's expand the table above into individual weeks and show progress in terms of earned value, with some illustrative delays to show how this works.

Table 7.2   Weekly earned value for *Grand Designs* example

Description of value delivered	Week	Budget	Cumulative budget	Earned value	Cumulative earned value
	1		£2,500	£0	£0.00
Toilet	2	£5,000	£5,000	£5,000	£5,000.00
	3		£8,333	£0	£5,000.00
	4		£11,667	£0	£5,000.00
Bathroom	5	£10,000	£15,000	£0	£5,000.00
	6		£18,750	£10,000	£15,000.00
	7		£22,500	£0	£15,000.00
	8		£26,250	£0	£15,000.00
Bedroom 1	9	£15,000	£30,000	£0	£15,000.00
	10		£36,000	£0	£15,000.00
	11		£42,000	£15,000	£30,000.00
	12		£48,000		
	13		£54,000		
Kitchen	14	£30,000	£60,000		

The earned value column shows when the value has been earned. The toilet, for example, was scheduled to be completed at the end of week two and we can see that its value of £5,000 was earned at the end of week two. It is on schedule. The bathroom, however, was scheduled to be completed at the end of week five, but its value of £10,000 was not earned until the end of week six. It is behind schedule.

The approach taken here is that value is only earned when a scheduled item is delivered and available to be used. Something is either completed or not completed. It is completely objective, with no ambiguity. It does, however, have a drawback when plotted on a graph, as illustrated in Figure 7.3.

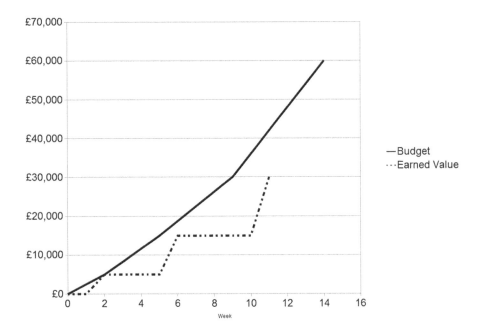

Figure 7.3   Earned value analysis with large increments of earned value

What we see is that there are big jumps in earned value when something is delivered. So, in week nine, for example, the graph might be a bit disconcerting, as it looks as if the project is way behind schedule.

SMOOTHING THE EARNED VALUE CURVE

The are two main ways of smoothing the earned value curve such that it reflects progress towards delivering value rather than taking big jumps as value as delivered:

1.   At the end of each reporting period (weeks in this example), the supplier estimates the proportion of work completed towards the value delivery.

2.   Value deliveries are broken down into constituent parts and these are used to report intermediate progress.

I think the second of these points is by far the most preferable, as it benefits from the same objectivity that applies to value delivery. Something tangible is either delivered or not delivered. It is measurable, whereas an estimate to complete is just an educated guess. So, for the bathroom, we might break it down something like this over the three time periods.

Table 7.3   Bathroom broken down into components, to smooth earned value curve, for *Grand Designs* example

Period	Deliverable	Cumulative Budget
1	Room built (walls, floor and ceiling)	£3,500
2	Plumbing complete and bathroom furniture installed	£8,000
4	Room decorated and lights installed	£10,000

Figure 7.4 opposite is what the graph might look like for our example if I add in the intermediate delivery of components.

Note that this approach also works well for projects that are not structured for regular value delivery. IT project plans are based on 'deliverables' (or 'products' in some organisations). 'Deliverables' include things like the designs, test plans or software for various parts of the system. An IT project of any significant duration will have lots of deliverables. You can ask your supplier to use the budgeted cost for each deliverable to produce an earned value analysis. The technique works just as well for large waterfall projects as it does for regular value delivery. This is no surprise as the technique originates from large construction projects.

The alternative approach is to use the percentage of work completed at each stage to plot intermediate points on the graph. For example, the budget for the bathroom is £10,000. It was estimated that it would take three weeks, but it actually took four. If the team is asked, during the first week, what proportion of the work has been completed, you might reasonably expect them to estimate that it is one-third (33 per cent) and an earned value of £3,333 would be added to the graph.

At the end of the second week, they would be asked the same question. If they are on schedule, they will answer two-thirds (66 per cent), so a further £3,333 would be added to the graph. If they realise they are behind schedule, they might say they think they are halfway (50 per cent), so only a further £1,667 would be added as earned value.

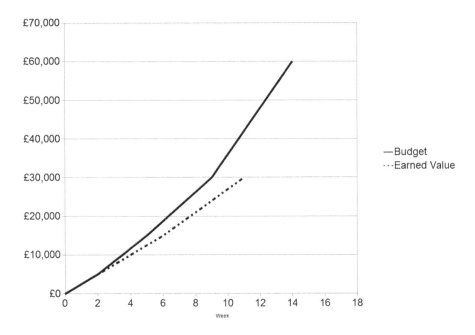

Figure 7.4   Earned value analysis with smoothed earned value

The problem with this approach is that it relies on a subjective estimate of percentage completed which is often wrong. The kitchen is built over three weeks, so it must be pretty obvious that it is behind schedule at the end of week two. However, I have seen plenty of IT projects where a delivery is scheduled to take three time periods (weeks or months) and it is reported as on schedule at the end of the first two periods, before the team admits defeat somewhere during the third period.

Take the kitchen, for example, which is budgeted at £30,000, over five reporting periods. If it was going to overrun, at what point would that become visible and, just as importantly, acknowledged and accepted by the project manager? My experience of IT projects is that it would not be apparent to the business manager until the fifth week, or the fourth at the earliest. This is not because of any intentional deception. As we saw earlier, people have an optimism bias and overestimate their ability to claw back lost time. This is often accompanied by the rationalisation that 'we have had a few hiccups but these are now behind us and it is plain sailing from hereon in'. IT projects are notorious for having deliverables that remain at 80 per cent completed for some considerable time.

HOW MUCH WORK IS NEEDED TO COMPLETE?

Asking how much work is needed to complete something yields a better answer than asking what proportion has been completed. It gets us to think about what needs to be done rather than what has been done and seems to produce more realistic responses.

ADDING ACTUAL COST TO THE GRAPH

The final element to add to the graph is the actual cost. Note that this is not the same as the earned value. To illustrate this, let's take the example of the toilet. Remember that it was budgeted at £5,000 and was delivered on time. Let's say, however, that the client changed their mind and decided to go for a more expensive suite and finish. What was budgeted at £5,000 has now cost £7,000 to deliver. The cost exceeds the budget, but the earned value when it is completed is still only £5,000. Earned value is expressed in terms of the original budgeted cost.

To round out the example, I have added in some cost overruns into the table below. I have only shown cumulative values in order to keep it manageable on the page.

Table 7.4   Data for earned value graph, including actual cost, for *Grand Designs* example

Week	Cumulative budget	Cumulative earned value	Cumulative actual cost
1	£2,500	£2,500	£2,500
2	£5,000	£5,000	£7,000
3	£8,333	£5,000	£11,000
4	£11,667	£8,500	£15,000
5	£15,000	£13,000	£19,000
6	£18,750	£15,000	£22,000
7	£22,500	£18,000	£27,000
8	£26,250	£21,000	£31,000
9	£30,000	£24,000	£34,500
10	£36,000	£27,000	£41,500
11	£42,000	£30,000	£49,500
12	£48,000		
13	£54,000		
14	£60,000		

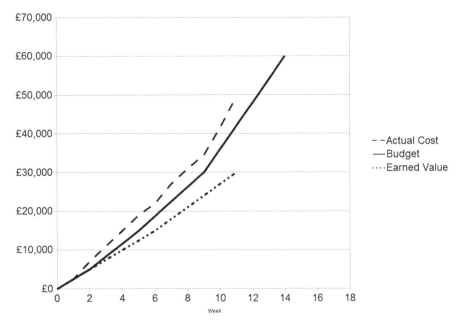

Figure 7.5   Earned value analysis with budget, actual and earned value

Figure 7.5 shows what it looks like on a single graph, reprised from the beginning of the chapter, showing that the project is both behind schedule and over budget.

FORECASTING COST AND TIME TO COMPLETE

As should be pretty obvious, earned value analysis can also help to reforecast the cost and schedule to needed to complete the project. One way of doing this is to simply take a ruler and extend the trend lines for actual cost and earned value and see where they end up. This can elicit surprisingly emotional responses from suppliers, who dismiss it as a crude, blunt instrument that takes no account of plans and the ability to claw time back.

An alternative is what I call the reality check approach. This assumes that the remaining items will run to their original budget and cost and this is added to the current position. In our example, the remaining item is the kitchen, which was estimated to take five weeks and to cost £30,000. This is added to the current position which was the actual cost at week 11. I will assume that the budget is evenly distributed over the five weeks at a rate of £6,000 per week.

Table 7.5   Adding in reality check 'forecast to complete' for *Grand Designs*
example

Week	Cumulative budget	Cumulative earned value	Cumulative forecast earned value	Cumulative forecast cost	Cumulative forecast cost
11	£42,000	£30,000		£49,500	
12	£48,000		£36,000		£55,500
13	£54,000		£42,000		£61,500
14	£60,000		£48,000		£67,500
15			£52,000		£73,500
16			£60,000		£79,500

The table shows that the project will be two weeks later than planned and
£19,500 over budget, unless the remaining work is done more quickly and
cheaply than originally planned. In this example, of course, it doesn't need a
table or graph to make the forecast – a quick sum would have sufficed. But in a
complex project with multiple deliverables, a graph can be of great assistance.
For the record, see our example with the reality check forecast added (see
Figure 7.6).

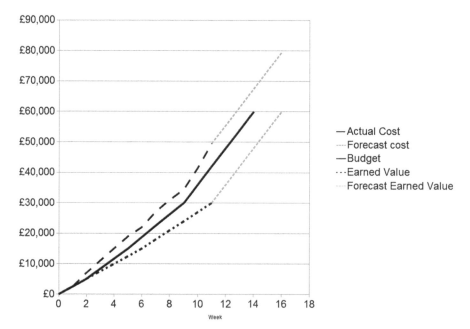

Figure 7.6   Earned value analysis with forecasts for actual and earned
value

The final way of reforecasting is to use the productivity performance for work already completed to predict the cost and duration of work yet to be done. In week 11, the project has spent £49,500 versus a budget of £42,000, which is an overspend of nearly 18 per cent. Similarly, our earned value is £30,000 versus a budget of £42,000, which is an underachievement of 29 per cent. These variation percentages can be applied to the uncompleted work in order to calculate the reforecast cost and schedule.

If you have adopted a regular value delivery strategy, this is the method you should ask your supplier to use. Each value delivery is a microcosm of the overall project, so it is reasonable to use it as a predictor of future performance. I think that it's worth reiterating what I said in Chapter 4. For an IT project, using regular value delivery, it is largely the same team that carries out design, build, test and implementation activities for each successive value delivery. And, broadly speaking, they will be using the same tools, in the same environment, with the same customer. It is reasonable, therefore, to use past productivity performance within the project as a good basis for forecasting future performance.

This is a less reasonable method of forecasting for a waterfall project because different teams will be working at different stages on deliverables that are not comparable. One cannot, for example, compare the productivity of the team writing software with that of the team testing it. They are very different activities and almost certainly comprise different people. This inability to extrapolate performance and learn from experience of delivery is one of the weaknesses of a waterfall approach. For waterfall projects, earned value analysis helps to identify when things as going awry, but, as current productivity is not a good indicator of future productivity, it isn't possible to reforecast with any great accuracy. However, experience shows that when early stages overrun, so do later ones.

Avoiding Earned Value Analysis Complacency

The rigour of earned value analysis can lull you into thinking that the graph is telling you all that you need to know about progress and expenditure. I am, however, recommending it to you as a tool that enables you to ask questions rather than as one that gives you the answers. What it tells you will depend on how it is applied by your supplier and that is why I have, in this chapter, emphasised the description of how it is calculated.

However, just in case you skimmed over the detail, below are the questions that you should ask yourself and your supplier when you are looking at an earned value analysis.

EARNED VALUE ANALYSIS QUESTIONS

- Is the analysis based on the completion of individual deliverables/products or on the estimated proportion completed? If the latter, how is this estimated?
- Do the calculations include a true *forecast to complete* deliverables/products, not just the actual cost to date deducted from the original estimate?
- How often are reforecasts made?
- Have any estimates to complete been reduced to mitigate overspend elsewhere?
- What is the cause of overspend or underspend?
- Why has more or less value been earned than predicted?
- Do reforecasts take account of the actual productivity levels on this project?
- How is contingency for unplanned work and change shown?

Keep in mind that the actual analysis is likely to be carried out by someone in the supplier's 'Project Management Office'. There is a reasonable possibility that your supplier's account manager, or indeed their project manager, will not know exactly how the numbers are calculated. Don't be fobbed off; you need to check. Pick a critical or large deliverable/product and get you supplier to walk you through the calculation. Let them know that you will want to undertake this sort of sampling, now and again, just to check your understanding. This will drive them down into the detail, so that they understand it, and it will also give you some assurance by relating to the graphs with things you can identify.

Key Issues Not Covered Already

Projects always have issues that demand immediate attention; that's what makes them issues rather than risks. Sometimes, however, it is difficult to determine whether an issue is truly project-threatening or whether it is just a buck being passed up the chain of command. And, if you establish an open risk reporting culture, as I have suggested, you can find a lot of low-level issues and risks arriving at your formal monthly meeting.

I have seen many formal review meetings get so mired in issues that seem pressing and immediate that they never get around the strategic considerations that will determine the success or otherwise of the project. Therefore, I prefer to leave consideration of issues that do not originate from the other agenda items until the end of the meeting. This ensures that senior management time is focused on what is strategically important.

What I find, if one takes this approach, is that key strategic issues usually arise from the scheduled agenda items of the business case summary, the risk review and the earned value analysis. And if they don't, the genuinely high-priority items can be addressed in the time that remains. The rest can usually be addressed by the project team meetings.

Key Points from this Chapter

- Show leadership throughout the project – leadership doesn't end when the ship sets sail.

- Regular value delivery and steering meetings are the key touchpoints to keep the project on target.

- Steering meetings should review the business case summary, risks and progress, and be about making decisions and taking action, not just sharing information.

- Actual cost versus budget and progress versus schedule can be displayed on a single earned value analysis graph.

- Earned value analysis is a good basis for identifying cost and schedule trends and making forecasts.

- It is important to ensure that regular team meetings are dealing with risks and issues.

WHAT IF YOUR PROJECT IS ALREADY WELL UNDER WAY?

It should be clear that all of the tools described in this chapter can be applied straight away. Even if you feel that creating a business case summary is a bridge too far, you can still create a monthly, or weekly, agenda that addresses each of the items.

If you don't have a list of key risks, issues, assumptions and performance criteria that you are tracking, with fresh actions against them, your project's heart isn't beating and you need to do something to rectify this pretty quickly.

In addition, ask yourself the following questions:

- Are roles and responsibilities and clear and widely communicated?
- What is the NPV?
- What are the assumptions underlying the NPV? Are they still valid? When will you know?
- Do you know how much you have spent and how much value it has delivered?
- Are you being a demanding customer?
- Are you having regular reviews that are more than a dog and pony show?

8

Conclusion: A Team of Leaders

At the beginning of this book, I asserted that poor business leadership is the major cause of IT project failure. Therefore, having devoted the last few chapters to practical tools, I want to close by returning to the topic of leadership.

For small projects, you will know all the stakeholders, all of the members of the project team and most of the IT supplier's team. You are able to have direct contact with almost everyone on the project. However, many projects are too large to establish and maintain a level of personal contact. The success of larger projects depends on having leaders, who share your vision, in the centres of expertise that are spread across the business functions, the IT supplier and partners outside the organisation.

When I start working with a client, they often ask me to have a look around and tell them how I think their project is going. I like to start this task informally, without looking at any paperwork, by having off-the-record chats with key members of the various teams. This does, of course, include people in formal management roles, but the people I really like to talk to are those below that level – the key doers and influencers with specific skills and knowledge.

What I often find is people who are keen to be part of a successful project but feel frustrated and stifled – not listened to and undervalued. These are often experienced people whose particular expertise is well respected by their peers. They usually have a long list of things that are being done wrong or could go wrong. These are your leaders in waiting and your challenge is to harness them.

To help you harness your leaders in waiting, I will use a sporting analogy to illustrate what I mean. After that, I will share a practical idea from the Harvard Business School Professor of Leadership and change guru, John Kotter. It's something you could implement tomorrow and make a difference, independently of anything else in this book.

The New Zealand All Blacks

The All Blacks are New Zealand's national Rugby Union team. They are arguably the most successful national sports team of all time. They have won 75 per cent of all the matches that they have ever played and have a winning record over every other side that they have played.[1] Only the mighty South African Springboks have run them close, but the All Blacks have still won 57 per cent of all of the matches played between them. The record of other teams against the All Blacks is much worse. Of all the matches ever played between them, the All Blacks have won against the major rugby nations by the following percentages: Australia (68 per cent), France (74 per cent), England (77 per cent), Wales (89 per cent) and Ireland (96 per cent).

The All Blacks are the current world champions, the acknowledged thought leaders in the game and the standard against which all other nations measure themselves. It is always a shock when they lose and is a source of great jubilation for those who manage to defeat them. The population of New Zealand is just under 5.5 million, just over half that of London. The All Blacks are doing something right and a large part of their success is what they refer to as 'leaders all over the park'.

Rugby Union is a complicated game, played by two teams of 15 players, comprised of eight 'forwards' and seven 'backs'. Each player has his or her own specialism. The game includes two static set pieces that are used to restart the game. The 'scrum' sees two sets of 'forwards' pushing against each other with all their might in order to gain possession of the ball. The 'line-out' sees that same set of 'forwards' jumping high into the air, against each other, in an effort to win the ball. Once the game is restarted, it can look like brutal chaos, with people running at speed, getting knocked down and then others piling into and onto each other in groups as they struggle for possession of the ball. Each 'phase' of the game has its own rules and requires a different set of skills. Unlike American Football, the same sets of players do the attacking, defending and kicking.

A rugby team has only one formal leader – the designated captain. If the captain is in the backs, he usually has a deputy in the forwards, known as the pack leader. But the All Blacks, always the innovators, were the first to take this a step further. Guided by a shared vision of how they wanted to play the game, they encouraged their more experienced, highly regarded players to take leadership roles during different phases and situations of the game.

Younger or less-experienced players would look to them, learn and seek to emulate their particular skills. More importantly, the leaders are the cool heads that take charge when the going gets tough, making crucial decisions on behalf of the team. Nowadays, each top rugby team talks about the need to develop leaders 'all over the park'.

Leaders All Over the Project

The analogy between a game of Rugby Union and an IT project is that each goes through different stages and complex situations, where different skills and experience are needed. And just like rugby, the formal leader is either often not present to make a decision or doesn't actually possess the right skills and experience to make that decision. Project decisions may not need to be made as quickly as in a game of rugby but brisk and confident decision making builds and maintains a project's momentum.

Therefore, I encourage you to think about who might be the natural leaders on your project. Who are the influencers and subject-matter experts that others look to for guidance? Who do you need to wield influence at certain stages and in particular topics? When you have identified these leaders, ensure that you chat to them on a regular basis as individuals or as a group. Let them know how much you value their contribution and leadership. But go a step further and follow the example of the All Blacks: tell them that you see them as important leaders on the project, with a reciprocal expectation that they will lead on your behalf.

If you can develop a network of informal leaders all over the project, they will act as the glue that keeps a project on track when things go wrong and processes fail for reasons beyond your control. Even if you lose a crucial 'player', you will have a strong team of leaders to guide you home.

A DUAL OPERATING SYSTEM

In 1995, John Kotter published an article in the *Harvard Business Review* entitled 'Leading Change: Why Transformation Efforts Fail'.[2] He followed it up with the bestselling book *Leading Change*[3] and became one of the most often-quoted sources of wisdom with regard to organisational change. He set out the following eight-stage process for successful change:

1.   Establishing a sense of urgency.

2.   Creating the guiding coalition.

3.   Developing a vision and strategy.

4.   Communicating the change vision.

5.   Empowering employees for broad-based action.

6.   Generating short-term wins.

7.   Consolidating gains and producing more change.

8.   Anchoring new approaches in the culture.

At the time that he was writing, he envisaged that the steps would be followed in sequence so as to achieve a specific change. However, in November 2012, he returned to the *Harvard Business Review*[4] to argue that the sequential approach was no longer adequate to meet the demands of modern business:

> *But the old ways of setting and implementing strategy are failing us. The hierarchical structures and organizational processes we have used for decades to run and improve our enterprises are no longer up to the task of winning in this faster-moving world.*

The solution, says Kotter, is for organisations to have a 'dual operating system': the existing, formal hierarchical structure and a parallel 'agile, network-like structure' made up of volunteers from different functions and levels, working together as equals. He states that:

> *This is not an 'either or' idea. It's 'both and'. I'm proposing two systems that operate in concert.*

In his article, Kotter recasts the sequential eight stages as eight simultaneously parallel accelerators:

1.   Create a sense of urgency around a single big opportunity.

2.   Build and maintain a guiding coalition.

3.   Formulate a strategic vision and develop change initiatives designed to capitalise on the big opportunity.

4.   Communicate the visions and strategy to create buy-in and attract a growing volunteer army.

5.   Accelerate movement towards the vision and the opportunity by ensuring that the network removes barriers.

6.   Celebrate visible, significant short-term wins.

7.   Never let up. Keep learning from experience. Don't declare victory too soon.

8.   Institutionalise strategic change in the culture.

A lot of what Kotter writes about concerning organisations chimes with the advice I have given you about projects. But what struck me most about this particular article was the idea that organisations need two parallel structures: one hierarchical and one networked. This is a similar idea to 'leaders all over the park', but goes a little further. The difference is that instead of simply nurturing and encouraging an informal team of leaders, Kotter advocates the establishment of a 'guiding coalition' and a 'volunteer army' on a more formal footing. His advice can clearly be applied to medium-sized to large projects, as well as organisations.

Since reading Kotter's article, I have tried out his approach with a couple of clients and it is having a positive impact. For one client, a particular problem manifested itself as a relationship problem between the business team and the IT supplier. This gave the client an opportunity to experiment with a parallel operating system. We convened the creation of a cross-functional team, including the supplier, to address the relationship problem which, incidentally, turned out to be a process problem. With the original problem under control, we encouraged the team to continue to meet every two weeks in order to identify and address critical issues and risks. After a short while, this 'guiding coalition' were meeting outside the fortnightly routine that we had established and had recruited members into 'sub-teams' to tackle specific issues. An expected side benefit was that day-to-day cross-functional collaboration increased significantly. It is now the norm to simply walk across the office and strike up a conversation with colleagues, rather than hide behind emails copied to multiple recipients, as so often happens.

Experiment to Learn

Like everything else in this book, Kotter's idea is something you can try out to see if it works for you. None of the tools in this book commits you to an irreversible course of action.

When you experiment, think about what you hope to learn before you experiment. Consider whether there are things that you can measure to determine how the experiment is going, while it is under way, and whether it was of value when completed. Even if you cannot measure things, it still helps to structure for learning by asking yourself:

> *What do I hope to achieve and learn by doing this?*

So, with the entreaty to 'just try it', we come to the end of the book. But if you want clarification, help or want to share your experiences with other readers, I have set up a place on my website where you can do so. I will also use that space to share new ideas and experiences that I think may interest and help you. So, good luck with your experiments and I hope to hear from you.

Join me at: www.doubleloopconsulting.com/value

Appendix A

Solution Workshops

The purpose of this appendix is to give you a range of tools that you can use to stimulate interaction in solution workshops. The framework for generating and evaluating options, within which these tools sit, is set out in Chapter 5.

The core input to a solution workshop is the shared project vision, plus key constraints and performance criteria; the richer the visions, the better. The tools described in Chapter 3 work particularly well as inputs to solution workshops:

- The movie poster.

- The cover story.

- Design the box.

- The TV advert or movie trailer.

Generating and Capturing Solution Ideas

AFFINITY MAP

An affinity map is a simple but effective way of getting solution ideas out on the table and grouping them together into themes. It works well with a relatively small number of people, say 15 or less, working face to face.

Ask participants to spend 10 minutes writing their solution ideas on Post-it notes. At the end of the 10 minutes, they are asked to stick the note on a vertical surface such as a wall or a whiteboard. This a better approach than brainstorming, where one goes around the room soliciting an idea from each person in turn, because it avoids the anchoring and framing effects that occur when one hears other people's ideas first.[1]

After posting their ideas, participants work together to group the notes into columns or clusters that are related to each other. Those that don't seem belong to any to group can be assigned to a 'parking lot' and reviewed at the end. Finally, ask the participants to give a name to each of the clusters and decide what to do with those in the parking lot. These clusters should then provide a good basis for a discussion on potential solutions.

There are a number of free Web-based applications that allow people to collaborate using virtual Post-it notes, so it is possible to do this remotely, although you would need to supplement it with video conferencing such as Skype or Google Hangouts. In addition, as virtual Post-it notes would be visible as they are posted, anchoring and framing effects would be in play.

The Affinity Map is widely credited[2] to Jiro Kawakita sometime in the 1960s, but I cannot find a reference to the original description.

BRAINWRITING

Brainwriting[3] is another tool that works well with small groups of people. It harnesses the knowledge that a lot of good ideas come from adding to or elaborating upon existing ones.

Participants are arranged in a circle and each is given a card or a sheet of paper to write on. Each participant writes a solution idea and hands it to the person to their left. Each person adds to the card by either elaborating upon the idea on the card or by adding another idea stimulated by the one on the card.

The cards are then passed on again for a specified number of times. Space on the cards is obviously limited, so the number of 'turns' is usually restricted to about three. Completed cards are taped to a whiteboard or flip-chart and participants are asked to put stars against those they like. The top ones are used a basis for discussing solutions.

The passing of ideas could easily be done remotely by using an email or forum software. The benefit of using the latter would be to leave the forums open for a remote discussion of ideas over the course of a fixed period, say a day or a week, removing the need for video conferencing. This would also be a way of opening the idea generation and discussion up to a much bigger group than is practical in a face-to-face scenario.

THE WORLD CAFÉ

The World Café is intended for large groups of over 20 people. A large range of support materials and information can be found at www.theworldcafe.com.

Creating a 'hospitable environment' is important. Ideally, it will look like a café, with a number of round tables, covered with chequered tablecloths, with flowers in the middle. Each table should have four chairs and certainly no more than five. It may tempting to dismiss this element as a bit silly and superfluous, but it is an important factor in getting people to interact, while thinking and feeling differently. If you have made the effort to get a lot of people together, then go the extra yard and try it. Tables should also be equipped with flip-charts, plenty of paper and coloured pens nearby.

It's important that the topic is very clear to all participants. In this case, the topic is 'solutions to achieve the vision'. I once saw a World Café with around 80 attendees, for a very large project, where the organisers had gone to the trouble of making a 'movie trailer' of the vision, together with loud swelling music. It was tongue-in-cheek, but it brought a smile to most people's faces and encouraged them to think in different ways.

The core of the approach is a series of 20-minute rounds in which each table discusses potential solutions. At the end of each round, everyone moves to a new table, leaving behind visible evidence of their ideas in the form of pictures and writing. A variation that I find works well is to leave one person at each table as the 'host' for the newcomers. The host's role is to summarise the discussion of the previous participants at the table. As you can see, the idea is one of cross-pollination. The number of rounds is entirely up to you and will depend on the size of the group, but three rounds is probably the minimum necessary to generate a good degree of interaction. When all of the rounds are finished, the ideas are 'harvested' and shared with the whole group for discussion.

If the group is very big and there are to be lots of rounds, you can choose to harvest in between rounds, but beware of the anchoring and framing effect described in the Affinity Map section above. Sharing is also clearly more of a challenge in a big group. One way of doing this is to create a 'gallery' of ideas on the wall and to start another series of rounds to evaluate those ideas.

I have never seen the World Café done remotely, so I cannot vouch for how successfully it works, but there is a link on www.theworldcafe.com to a partner who hosts online World Café events using teleconferencing technology.

Choosing a Solution Option

Once a range of solution ideas have been generated, you will want to use the workshops to flesh them out and evaluate them. I will give a brief reprise of things discussed in previous chapters and add a couple of additional tools that you might find useful. All of the tools described below could be used remotely using video or teleconferencing, but I believe that they work better when people are together in one place, at least initially.

PERFORMANCE CRITERIA MATRIX

In Chapter 5, I described in detail how to use a matrix to compare individual solution components. Here's a reminder of what an individual solution option might look like for a mobile phone.

Table A.1   Grouping of solution components into one solution option

	Sexy	Internet	Ease of use	Speed of use	Cost ($)
Virtual keyboard	90%		70%	70%	b
Touch-screen	100%		100%	100%	d
Glass screen	90%				e
Device specific applications	75%	75%	80%	80%	g
Optimised browser	30%	90%	20%	30%	h
Weight < 130 g	90%				j
Thickness < 12 mm	80%				k
Total coverage	555%	165%	270%	280%	(b+d+e+g+h+j+k)

Asking workshop participants to work together to complete this type of matrix, for each solution option, is an effective way of thinking through the relative merits of these options.

OVERALL SOLUTION MATRIX

You can use the overall solution matrix in conjunction with the performance criteria matrix above or on its own. Workshop participants score the five dimensions of cost, constraints, performance criteria, assumptions and risks on a scale from one to five. As with the performance criteria matrix, the process of thinking through the scoring for the relative importance and impact of the dimensions is more important than the numerical result.

Table A.2   Comparison of differing solution options

	Solution 1	Solution 2	Solution 3	Solution 4
Cost	4	3	3	1
Constraints	1	3	4	5
Performance criteria	2	4	4	4
Assumptions	1	3	2	4
Risks	5	4	3	2
Total	13	17	16	16

NEW, USEFUL AND FEASIBLE TEST

The New, Useful and Feasible (NUF) test is, according to *Gamestorming*,[4] an invaluable compendium of workshop tools, an adaptation of process used to evaluate patents. It is another type of impact matrix, but one designed specifically for launching a new product or service. Workshop participants score solution options across the three NUF dimensions on a scale of 1–10:

- New – things that are new to the customer or market score higher.

- Useful – the greater the coverage of the vision, the higher the score.

- Feasible – the lower the cost and technical difficulty, the higher the score.

Table A.3   Ranking solutions options by new, useful and feasible

	Solution 1	Solution 2	Solution 3	Solution 4
Novelty	5	7	8	4
Useful	6	5	7	8
Feasible	8	6	4	9
Total	19	18	19	21

As with the other matrices, the thinking process is more important that the actual result.

BUSINESS MODEL CANVAS

The Business Model Canvas[5] is a clever tool for thinking through solution options that will launch new businesses, services or products. With a bit of creativity, it can be used to think through business solutions for many types of project.

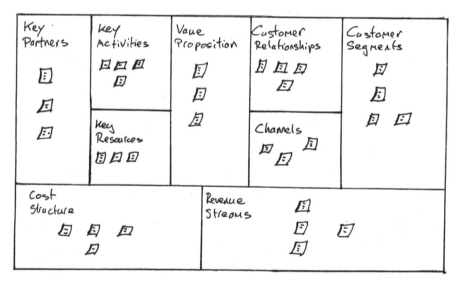

Figure A.1   Business Model Canvas

The Canvas is ideal for workshops and a poster for this purpose can be downloaded free of charge, under the Creative Commons licence, at www.

businessmodelgeneration.com/canvas. The website also contains a lot of advice on how to use the Canvas.

In a solution workshop, you can ask participants to use Post-it notes (which are easy to change and move) to populate each section, generating a different canvas for each of the different solution options. Then, to evaluate these options, you can ask participants to highlight each model's strengths and weaknesses by adding a plus or minus sign to each Post-it note. Or, better still, use different-coloured Post-it notes (red, yellow and green) to highlight the relative strength or weakness.

Once a solution option is chosen, the canvas is a great tool for fleshing out that solution in greater detail.

Appendix B

Glossary

The purpose of this glossary is primarily to collect, in one place, my definitions of terms used in the book. They are not intended as universally accepted definitions; they are simply what I mean when I use them in this book. The secondary purpose is to describe my interpretation, in business terms, of a few common IT terms that you might come across and may be useful to understand.

Assumptions

Assumptions can occur at any time during a project, but are most critical when developing a business case and the associated solution. Assumptions can be a numerical range or something that is either true or false. An example of the former might be: the operator of the solution has to become proficient, as measured by an objective test, in less than half a day. An example of the latter might be: railway stations are willing to create a space to set up a kiosk to serve homeless people. If key assumptions prove to be false, then the business case and hence the viability of the project should be reviewed.

Black Swan

The term 'black swan' was coined by Nassim Nicholas Taleb in his book *The Black Swan: The Impact of the Highly Improbable*. Taleb describes a black swan as an event that is 'outside the realm of regular expectations … carries an extreme impact … [and is] after the fact explainable and predictable'.

Cloud

The term 'cloud' is used by IT people in a variety of ways, but in essence it means that data and/or processing are stored and managed outside the organisation, and are usually accessed over the Internet. Cloud-based solutions have been made possible by the speed of publicly available networks, the advances in Web browsers and the language they use (HTML), and the development of mobile phones into powerful mobile computers. The term 'cloud' comes from the diagrams drawn by technical people, where a network connection is typically drawn as disappearing into a cloud.

Microsoft's Hotmail was an early example of a cloud solution. Nothing is stored locally. The software and the data are managed by Microsoft. Cloud solutions now exist for almost every application you can imagine, from personnel management and accounting through to a full music studio mixing desk. Typically, all one needs is a Web browser and an Internet connection. There are also cloud solutions for personal and corporate data, such as Dropbox and Rackspace.

The applications we now routinely use on our mobile devices such as phones and tablets are a form of cloud computing. Some are a hybrid with the software on the mobile device and the data in the cloud, but there appears to be a trend towards more and more of the software being in the cloud and being downloaded quickly to run and then deleted, just like in a Web browser.

The benefits of a cloud solution is that you don't have to invest in and manage infrastructure or software and, instead, just pay for what you use. The downside is that you have to trust someone else to manage applications and data that may be business-critical. If you are considering a cloud solution, a key consideration should be access to your data in the event that you wanted to change supplier or the supplier goes bust. If the solution isn't critical, then you may not be worried about this risk, but if it is critical, I would suggest you need a contingency plan.

Constraint

A constraint is something that limits choice. It can be imposed on the vision or the solution options to achieve the vision. An example of a constraint is that a project to provide drinking water is limited to rainwater harvesting. Other types of constraints are the budget or time available to achieve the vision.

IT Project

An IT project is a project that delivers a new or changed capability, based on IT, that delivers business value. The project is not complete until the value is realised or is demonstrably on the way to being realised.

IT Supplier

An IT supplier is an internal IT department, an external services supplier or a combination of both.

Net Present Value (NPV)

An NPV aggregates future cash flows and expresses them in today's money as a single number. This number shows how much financial value is added or subtracted by the project. The financial case should reflect the total cost of ownership, including post-project costs such as operating and license costs, rather than just the project development cost. See Appendix C for more information on this.

Performance Criteria

Performance criteria define what a solution has to deliver in terms of business or technical performance. An example of a business performance criteria is the number of operator errors made per person per day. A technical performance criterion might be the time that it takes to process a message such as a request go buy – this sort of thing is critical for stock exchanges and other types of financial exchanges. Performance criteria are most useful when they are quantified (see Chapter 5 for advice on how to do this).

Project Owner

If the project sponsor is the CEO, the project owner is the chairman. It isn't a necessary to have an 'owner', but when you have a designated sponsor who does not have sufficient time to devote to the project, you can suggest that they take on the role of owner and delegate sponsor responsibility to someone with more time. In way this, you still retain the influence of the owner to help manage senior stakeholders and to provide advice and guidance on key decisions.

Project Sponsor

The project sponsor is the person who wants the project and pays for it. The sponsor:

- wants the value delivered by the project;

- has agreed to spend the money to get that value;

- will champion the project throughout its life;

- will engage fully at the key touchpoints;

- will help the project team address obstacles outside their control;

- has the power to stop the project if it is not going to deliver the expected value.

Risks

Risks are things that could prevent the project from achieving its vision. Surfacing and dealing with risks throughout the project is one of the critical success factors for IT projects.

Shared Project Vision

A shared vision brings your project's outcome to life. It describes what the world will be like after the project has been delivered. It describes the value that people will see, hear and feel; the more that it goes beyond a static picture and engages senses and emotions, the more memorable and compelling it will be. A good vision acts as the true north for your project team.

Solution

If the vision describes *what* you want to achieve, a 'solution' describes, in business terms, *how* you will achieve it. It describes the role played by IT as part of the overall business solution, but it is not a technical specification of the IT component of the solution.

Stakeholder

A stakeholder is a person, a group of people or an organisation that can affect or be affected by a project. It is sometimes beneficial to extend this definition to inanimate things such as regulation and legislation. Stakeholders may be within your own organisation or outside of it. Customers are clearly stakeholders, but I usually list them separately because they often get left out when it comes to active shaping activities.

Sunk Cost

Although the term 'sunk cost' is sometimes used colloquially, it has a specific meaning in the context of a project's financial appraisal. Essentially, the sunk cost is money that has already been spent but cannot be recovered. The correct financial appraisal at any time in a project's life should therefore be based on future costs, without considering the sunk cost.

For example, let's say that we have a project that is estimated to cost £800,000 to deliver a financial benefit of £1.1 million at today's value. Assuming that risk has been taken into account, the project is worth doing. Now let's say we are halfway through the project, but have already spent £600,000. Also, let's say that it is now estimated that the project will cost another £700,000 to complete, bringing the total project cost to £1.3million. The total cost of the project now outweighs the benefit and it might be argued that the project should be stopped.

However, the principle of sunk costs says that the first £600,000 cannot be recovered and that the appraisal should be based on the money that needs to spent to deliver the benefit. In this instance, we need to spend an estimated £700,000 to deliver a benefit of £1.1 million. In strictly financial terms, the project is still viable. If, however, the true cost had been known at the outset, it may never have been approved. Whether the project can really be completed for £700,000, given its track record, and whether there are really £1.1 million of benefits are different matters.

Value

Value conveys a combination of both benefit and cost – or it is the bang for the buck. Value is in the eye of its beholders. If the only benefit conveyed by buying a Rolex was the ability to tell the time accurately, few would be sold. It is important, therefore, to engage with stakeholders to understand how they perceive value.

Appendix C

Net Present Value (NPV) Primer

In essence, an NPV aggregates future cash flows, of costs and benefits, and expresses them in today's money as a single number. This number shows how much financial value is added or subtracted by the project.

The key concept to understand is that of Present Value. The 'net' part of NPV is simply adding and subtracting a series of numbers to obtain a 'net' value, and we will come back to this later. So, for now, let me explain Present Value with a simple example.

Let's say you have £1,000. If you are able to invest it somewhere fairly safe at an annual interest rate of five per cent. After one year you will have £1,050. This is the equivalent of saying that £1,050 in a year's time has 'Present Value' of £1,000. And that's the core concept. By taking account of interest rates, we express a future amount of money in terms of what it is worth today.

To give another example, let's say that a benefactor gives you the choice between receiving either £900 today or £1,000 in a year's time. Which should you choose? You can answer this by calculating what the £900 would be worth in a year's time if you invested it today. For now, let's stick with an interest rate of five per cent. One year's interest on £900 is £45, so in a year's time you would have £945. That's less than the £1,000 you have been offered if you wait. So, unless you have a better use for the money today, such as a holiday that is only available this year, then you should wait for the £1,000 next year.

But because things get more complicated with projects and cash flows across multiple years, it is necessary to adopt the convention of expressing future value in terms of Present Value (as opposed to the other way around, as was the case in the preceding paragraph). Rather than asking what the £900 would be worth next year, we ask what the £1,000 in a year's time will be worth today (the Present Value). Staying with an interest rate of five per cent, the Present Value of £1,000 next year is £1,000 divided by the interest rate plus one:

$$PV = £1,000 / (1 + \text{Interest rate}) = £1,000 / (100\% + 5\%) = £1,000 / 1.05 = £952$$

So the Present Value is £952, which is better than the £900 on offer today. Unsurprisingly, it represents the same conclusion as projecting the £900 forward. The term we use to describe this calculation, from future value to Present Value, is 'discounting' and the rate that we used (five per cent in this case) is known as the 'discount rate'. We have discounted a future value of £1,000 to its Present Value of £952. If you have grasped this principle, you are home and dry. If not, I suggest you work through some simple examples of your own invention, moving values forwards and back again, using an interest rate.

Now let's take a more complicated example. Let's say that we have a project that is estimated to cost £1,000,000 in order to deliver an annual cost saving of £300,000. Is this a project worth doing? Here is what the cash flows from the project will look like over five years.

Table C.1   Project cash flow

	Year 0	Year 1	Year 2	Year 3	Year 4	Total
Cost	-£1,000,000					-£1,000,000
Income		£300,000	£300,000	£300,000	£300,000	£1,200,000
Net cash flow	-£1,000,000	£300,000	£300,000	£300,000	£300,000	£200,000

On the face of it, the project will generate a surplus of £200,000 in year 4, representing a return on investment of 20 per cent, which is not bad. I have seen this sort of calculation in many business cases. But, as we have seen, £300,000 next year is worth less than having that equivalent sum of money today. Using a discount rate of five per cent, the Present Value of £300,000 in year 1 is (300,000 / 1.05) which is £286,000.

What about the other years? Applying similar logic to the other years, we obtain the following results:

- £300,000 in year 1 is worth (£300,000 / 1.05) in year zero which is £285,714.

- £300,000 in year 2 is worth £285,714 in year 1,

  - so its value in year zero is (£285,714 / 1.05) which is £272,109.

- £300,000 in year 3 is worth £285,714 in year 2,

  - so its value in year 1 is (£285,714 / 1.05) which is £272,109,
  - so its value in year zero is (£272,109 / 1.05) which is £259,151.

- 300,000 in year 4 is worth £285,714 in year 3,

  - so its value in year 2 is (£285,714 / 1.05) which is £272,109,
  - so its value in year 1 is (£271,109 / 1.05) which is £259,151,
  - so its value in year zero is (£259,151 / 1.05) which is £246,811.

Totalling these year zeroes, together with the cost that occurred in year zero, gives us the Net Present Value of £63,785, which is calculated like this:

```
-£1,000,000
  +£285,714
  +£272,109
  +£259,151
  +£246,811
  _____

    £63,785
```

Given a discount rate of five per cent, the project adds £63,785 of value to the organisation. It's positive, but not as healthy as the apparent £200,000 that we started with. You don't need to carry out these sorts of long-winded calculations to figure that out. All of the popular spreadsheet software products have an NPV function that can do these calculations for you. The format is usually, something like '=NPV (DiscountRate, StartRange...EndRange)'. If you use this function, be careful not to discount the year zero values, which are already expressed in terms of Present Value; this is a very common mistake.

The NPV calculation is clearly sensitive to the discount rate used in the calculation. In the example that I have used above, the NPV starts to become negative at 7.75 per cent. And if I increase the rate to 10 per cent, the NPV is -£49,000. Try constructing the spreadsheet yourself and playing around with different values.

So what discount rate should you use? The answer is to ask your finance department or accountant, who will calculate value for your business based on its particular circumstances. Large organisations will certainly have a 'hurdle rate' defined for projects. My experience is that most large organisations use a figure of around 10 per cent, plus or minus two per cent. But should you be the type of person who doesn't like to take things at face value, here is some background on what is appropriate.

The discount rate, which is also known as the 'hurdle rate' or the 'opportunity cost of capital', is 'the rate offered by comparable investment alternatives'.[1] In other words, it is the rate of return you might get if you used the money to do something else which is *comparable*. Now, as we know from the data presented in Chapter 1, investment in IT projects is risky. Using a rate that is derived from safe investments such as government securities is clearly inappropriate. Perhaps buying shares in a technology company is more comparable? It's a judgement, not science.

I have heard some people suggest using something called the Weighted Average Cost of Capital (WACC). This is essentially the overall cost of financing the business based on shares, bonds and other forms of borrowing for your specific company. To give you an idea of the sort of rates we are talking about, we can look at data published by New York University. In January 2012,[2] the University calculated that the average WACC, across all sectors of insustry, was 7.05 per cent.

The highest figure was for semiconductor equipment, which was 11.46 per cent, and the lowest was for water utilities, which was 3.91 per cent. This reflects the relative riskiness of these industries for investors and lenders. It does not, however, reflect the riskiness of individual projects within these industries. Is an IT project in a water utility a lesser risk that one in advertising which has a WACC of 11.42 per cent? It's unlikely. WACC by industry does not therefore appear to be the answer, though the average WACC adjusted for risk could be a starting point. So the answer is to ask your finance expert, but do challenge them to ensure that the rate they suggest is commensurate with the project risk and not just the company's WACC.

Incidentally, you might be thinking that the value of future cash flows is affected by inflation as well as interest rates. This is true, but the interest rate effectively incorporates the effect of inflation. If you look at some historical graphs of interest and inflation rates,[3] you will see that they move up and down together.

With respect to the appropriate time horizon, the more years of positive cash flow that one adds to the NPV calculation, the better the final number will look. My experience, however, is that most organisations use a three- or five-year time horizon for IT projects on the basis that cash flows beyond this timeframe are unpredictable. However, as with the discount rate, there is no correct answer. It comes down to a judgement about the certainty (or, to put it another way, the riskiness) of future cash flows.

Using an NPV to evaluate the financial viability of your project is not an exact science. It depends on a number of assumptions about costs, value delivered, discount rates and time horizons. Too often, a single number is calculated and used to justify the project, sometimes by tweaking just a few key spreadsheet cells here and there to give 'the right answer'. Used intelligently, however, NPV is a powerful tool for modelling different combinations of assumptions. If you keep these numbers visible, test them and review them regularly, then an NPV model will serve you well.

References

Introduction

1. The Standish Group International Inc., *The CHAOS Report (1994)*, 1995; *CHAOS Manifesto, 2010*; See http://www.bcs.org/content/ConWebDoc/ 19584 [accessed 20 January 2012].
2. The Standish Group International Inc., *CHAOS Manifesto, 2010*; See http:// www.ogc.gov.uk/documents/cp0015.pdf [accessed 20 January 2012].
3. Kahneman, D., *Thinking Fast and Slow.* London: Penguin, 2011.
4. Sharot, T., *The Optimism Bias.* London: Constable & Robinson, 2012.

Chapter 1

1. The Standish Group International Inc., *The CHAOS Report (1994)*, 1995.
2. The Standish Group International Inc., *CHAOS Manifesto, 2010*.
3. See http://www.computer.org/portal/c/document_library/get_file?uu id984758f1-4f03-4609-afe6-1c2e4df31900&groupId=889147 [accessed 1 January 2012].
4. See http://www.bcs.org/content/ConWebDoc/19584 [accessed 20 January 2012].
5. Flyvbjerg, B. and Budzier, A., 'Why Your IT Project May Be Riskier Than You Think', *Harvard Business Review*, September 2011.
6. Taleb, N.N., *The Black Swan: The Impact of the Highly Improbable*. London: Penguin, 2008.
7. See http://www.information-age.com/articles/292891/sainsburys-dogged-by-supply-chain-problems.thtmlply-chain-IT-trouble-hits-profit [accessed 20 January 2012]; See http://www.supplymanagement.com/analysis/ features/2004/digital-disaster [accessed 20 January 2012].
8. See http://spectrum.ieee.org/computing/software/who-killed-the-virtual-case-file [accessed 20 January 2012]; See http://www.justice.gov/oig/ testimony/0502/final.pdf [accessed 20 January 2012].

9.   See http://www.ft.com/cms/s/0/00a2c4b0-191f-11db-b02f-0000779e2340.
      html#axzz2AgSUoLn4 [accessed 20 January 2012]; See http://www.
      computerweekly.com/news/2240065826/Did-lack-of-IT-involvement-at-
      outset-doom-LCHClearnets-grand-vision [accessed 20 January 2012].
10.   Sharot, T., *The Optimism Bias.* London: Constable & Robinson, 2012.
11.   Kahneman, D., *Thinking Fast and Slow.* London: Penguin, 2011.
12.   Carr, N.G., 'IT Doesn't Matter', *Harvard Business Review,* May 2003.

Chapter 2

1.   The Standish Group International Inc., *CHAOS Manifesto, 2010.*
2.   See http://www.bcs.org/category/11280 [accessed 20 January 2012].
3.   See http://www.it-cortex.com/Stat_Failure_Cause.htm#The%20OASIG
      %20Study%20(1995) [accessed 20 January 2012].
4.   See http://www.ogc.gov.uk/documents/cp0015.pdf [accessed 20 January
      2012].
5.   See http://www.parliament.uk/documents/post/pr200.pdf [accessed 20
      January 2012].
6.   See http://dl.acm.org/citation.cfm?id=1289670 [accessed 20 January 2012].
7.   See http://www.it-cortex.com/Stat_Failure_Cause.htm#The%20KPMG%
      20Canada%20Survey%20(1997) [accessed 20 January 2012].
8.   See http://www.fr.capgemini.com/m/fr/doc/POV_SurveyBT_13FLRE.pdf
      [accessed 20 January 2012].
9.   See http://spectrum.ieee.org/computing/software/who-killed-the-virtual-
      case-file [accessed 1 November 2012].
10.   See http://www.justice.gov/oig/testimony/0502/final.pdf [accessed 1
      November 2012].
11.   See http://www.publications.parliament.uk/pa/cm201012/cmselect/cm
      pubacc/1070/107004.htm [accessed 1 November 2012].
12.   See http://www.information-age.com/articles/292891/sainsburys-dogged-
      by-supply-chain-problems.thtmlply-chain-IT-trouble-hits-profit
      [accessed 1 November 2012].
13.   See http://www.j-sainsbury.co.uk/media/276176/interims01slides_spd.pdf
      [accessed 1 November 2012].
14.   See http://www.j-sainsbury.co.uk/media/219563/slide_davis.pdf [accessed
      1 November 2012].
15.   See http://www.supplymanagement.com/analysis/features/2004/digital-
      disaster [accessed 1 November 2012].
16.   See http://www.computerweekly.com/news/2240058411/Sainsburys-writes
      -off-260m-as-supply-chain-IT-trouble-hits-profit [accessed 1 November
      2012].

17. See http://www.telegraph.co.uk/finance/2924771/Sainsburys-ends-2.1bn-IT-contract.html [accessed 1 November 2012].
18. Kahneman, D., *Thinking Fast and Slow*. London: Penguin, 2011.
19. See http://www.linkedin.com/groupItem?view=&gid=69172&type=member&item=88995532&trk=group_search_item_list-0-b-ttl&goback=%2Egna_69172 [accessed 1 November 2012].
20. See http://blog.standishgroup.com/news [accessed 17 July 2012]; See http://www.asugnews.com/2012/07/16/project-management-success-a-skilled-executive-sponsor-needed [accessed 17 July 2012].

Chapter 3

1. Taiichi, O., *Toyota Production System: Beyond Large-Scale Production*. Tokyo: Productivity Inc., 1988.
2. Spradlin, D., 'Are You Solving the Right Problem?', *Harvard Business Review*, September 2012.
3. See http://www.who.int/water_sanitation_health/diseases/burden/en [accessed 5 November 2012].
4. See http://store.grove.com/s.nl/c.ACCT75322/sc.2/category.2100/.f [accessed 5 November 2012].
5. Gray, D. et al., *Gamestorming*. Sebastapol, O'Reilly Media Inc., 2010.
6. See http://www.sony.net/SonyInfo/CorporateInfo/History/SonyHistory/2-05.html [accessed 5 November 2012].
7. Kahneman, D., *Thinking Fast and Slow*. London: Penguin, 2011.
8. Senge, P., *The Fifth Discipline*. London: Century Business, 1993.
9. See http://www.mitpressjournals.org/doi/pdf/10.1162/itgg.2007.2.1-2.63 [accessed 5 November 2012].
10. See http://appleinsider.com/articles/12/02/03/former_apple_product_manager_recounts_how_jobs_motivated_first_iphone_team.html [accessed 5 November 2012].
11. Isaacson, W., *Steve Jobs: The Exclusive Biography*. New York: Simon & Schuster, 2012.

Chapter 4

1. Sharot, T., *The Optimism Bias*. London: Constable & Robinson, 2012.
2. Brooks, F.P., *The Mythical Man-Month*. Boston, MA: Addison-Wesley, 1995.
3. The Standish Group International Inc., *CHAOS Manifesto, 2010*.
4. See http://weblog.erenkrantz.com/~jerenk/phase-ii/Boe88.pdf [accessed 1 December 2012].

5.   See http://www.agilealliance.org/the-alliance/the-agile-manifesto [accessed 1 December 2012].

6.   Reinersten, D. and Thonke, S., 'Six Myths of Product Development', *Harvard Business Review*, May 2012.

7.   Womack, D., Jones, D. and Roos, D., *The Machine That Changed the World*. London: Simon & Schuster, 1990.

8.   See http://www.cardiff.ac.uk/lean/principles/index.html [accessed 1 December 2012].

9.   The Standish Group International Inc., *CHAOS Manifesto, 2010*.

Chapter 5

1.   Kahneman, D., *Thinking Fast and Slow*. London: Penguin, 2011.

2.   Ibid.

3.   Wilson, T.D., *Strangers to Ourselves*. Cambridge, MA: Belknap Press, 2002.

4.   Gilb, T., *Principles of Software Engineering Management*. Boston, MA: Addison-Wesley, 1988.

5.   Ishikawa, K., *Guide to Quality Control*. Tokyo: JUSE Press, 1968.

6.   Klein, G., 'Performing a Project Premortem', *Harvard Business Review*, September 2007.

7.   Gilb, T., *Principles of Software Engineering Management*. Boston, MA: Addison-Wesley, 1988.

8.   Carr, N.G., 'IT Doesn't Matter', *Harvard Business Review*, May 2003.

Chapter 6

1.   Kahneman, D., *Thinking Fast and Slow*. London: Penguin, 2011.

2.   Ibid.

3.   Gawande, A., *The Checklist Manifesto: How to Get Things Right*. London, Profile Books, 2010.

Chapter 7

1.   Drucker, P., 'What Makes an Effective Executive', *Harvard Business Review*, June 2004.

Chapter 8

1.   See http://stats.allblacks.com [accessed 1 January 2013].

2.   Kotter, J.P., 'Leading Change: Why Transformation Efforts Fail', *Harvard Business Review*, March–April 1995.

3.   Kotter, J.P., *Leading Change*. Cambridge, MA: Harvard Business School Press, 1996.
4.   Kotter, J.P., 'Accelerate', *Harvard Business Review*, November 2012.

Appendix A

1.   Kahneman, D., *Thinking Fast and Slow*. London: Penguin, 2011.
2.   Gray, D. et al., *Gamestorming.* Sebastapol: O'Reilly Media Inc., 2010.
3.   Michalko, M., *Thinkertoys: A Handbook of Creative Thinking*. Berkeley: Ten Speed Press, 1991.
4.   Gray, D. et al., *Gamestorming.* Sebastapol: O'Reilly Media Inc., 2010.
5.   Osterwalder, A. and Pigneur, Y., *Business Model Generation,* Hoboken: John Wiley & Sons Inc., 2010.

Appendix C

1.   Brearly, R.A. and Myers, S.C., *Principles of Corporate Finance.* New York: McGraw-Hill, 1991.
2.   See   http://w4.stern.nyu.edu/~adamodar/New_Home_Page/datafile/wacc. htm [accessed 22 December 2012].
3.   See   http://econ.economicshelp.org/2009/04/link-between-inflation-and-interest.html [accessed 22 December 2012].

Index

performance criteria 94–5, 144–5
risk **90**, 90–91, 120–21, **121**
meetings *see* review meetings;
  team meetings
Microsoft 79, 150
Millennium Development Goals 43–4
missions 37–8, 50, 52
Morita, Akio 41
movie posters 40, 141
movie trailers 41, 141, 143

National Audit Office (NAO) 19
National Health Service (NHS) 22–3
needs 37–8, 52
Net Present Value (NPV) 104–6, 107,
  113, 134, 151, 155–9
New, Useful and Feasible (NUF) test
  145–6
New Zealand All Blacks 136–7
novelty of projects **57**, 57–8, 61

off-the-shelf solutions 11–12, 15, 82,
  97
Office of Government Commerce
  (OGC) 19
offshore suppliers 66–7
Ohga, Norio 41
Olympic Games 85, 91–2
one-minute health-check 3–4
optimism bias 3, 10, 127
Organisational Aspects Special
  Interest Group (OASIG) 19
organisational change 137–9
organisational culture 24, 121, 132
overall solution matrices 145
overruns 5–9, 16, 18, 56–8, 61, 105

performance criteria
  in the business case summary
    106–7, **107**, 113

definition 151
evaluating against delivery 34, 116,
  117
identifying 80–84
quantifying 81–4, 97, 107
and solution option evaluation
  93–5, 144–5
and solution option generation
  34, 73, 80–84, 92–3, 97–8, 141
performance criteria matrices 94–5,
  144–5
pilot solutions 85, 86–7
pre-mortems 89
present value 155–6
problem-solving 38, 58
problems 37–8, 52
project cancellations 5, 6, 7, 8, 103,
  104
project culture 24, 121, 132
project delivery 30, 34, 115–34; *see
  also* regular value delivery
project failures 5–9, **8**, 19–24, **33**
project managers 2, 111, 119
project novelty **57**, 57–8, 61
project overruns 5–9, 16, 18, 56–8, 61,
  105
project owners 28, 29–30, 31, 151
project requirements
  changing 20, 22, 64, 65, 67
  defining 30, 61–2, 63, 65, 66–7
  not well defined 20, 22
  solution does not meet 18, 23
project selection 27–8
project scope 110, 112, 113
project size 10–11, **11**
project sponsors 1, 2, 27–31, 110, 117,
  118–19, 151–2
project roles 24–5, 27–31, 110–11
project team meetings 119, 133, 139
project vision *see* vision

For Product Safety Concerns and Information please contact our
EU representative GPSR@taylorandfrancis.com Taylor & Francis
Verlag GmbH, Kaufingerstraße 24, 80331 München, Germany